AF574905

Modern World Leaders

Ban Ki-moon

Modern World Leaders

Michelle Bachelet
Ban Ki-moon
Tony Blair
Gordon Brown
George W. Bush
Felipe Calderón
Hugo Chávez
Jacques Chirac
Hu Jintao
Hamid Karzai
Ali Khamenei
Kim Jong Il
Thabo Mbeki
Angela Merkel
Hosni Mubarak
Pervez Musharraf
Ehud Olmert
Pope Benedict XVI
Pope John Paul II
Roh Moo Hyun
Vladimir Putin
Nicolas Sarkozy
The Saudi Royal Family
Ariel Sharon
Viktor Yushchenko

Modern World Leaders

Ban Ki-moon

Rebecca Aldridge

Ban Ki-moon

For information, contact:

Chelsea House
An imprint of Infobase Publishing
132 West 31st Street
New York, NY 10001

Library of Congress Cataloging-in-Publication Data
Aldridge, Rebecca.
Ban Ki-Moon / by Rebecca Aldridge.
p. cm. — (Modern world leaders)
Includes bibliographical references and index.
ISBN 978-1-60413-070-6 (hbk. : alk. paper) 1. Pan, Ki-mun, 1944—Juvenile literature. 2. United Nations—Biography—Juvenile literature. 3. United Nations—History—Juvenile literature. 4. Statesmen—Korea (South)—Biography—Juvenile literature. I. Title.
D839.7.P36A67 2009
341.23092—dc22
[B] 2008026566

Chelsea House books are available at special discounts when purchased in bulk quantities for businesses, associations, institutions, or sales promotions. Please call our Special Sales Department in New York at (212) 967-8800 or (800) 322-8755.

You can find Chelsea House on the World Wide Web at http://www.chelseahouse.com

Text design by Erik Lindstrom
Cover design by Takeshi Takahashi

Printed in the United States of America

Bang EJB 10 9 8 7 6 5 4 3 2 1

This book is printed on acid-free paper.

Table of Contents

Arthur M. Schlesinger, Jr.

On Leadership

Leadership, it may be said, is really what makes the world go round. Love no doubt smoothes the passage; but love is a private transaction between consenting adults. Leadership is a public transaction with history. The idea of leadership affirms the capacity of individuals to move, inspire, and mobilize masses of people so that they act together in pursuit of an end. Sometimes leadership serves good purposes, sometimes bad; but whether the end is benign or evil, great leaders are those men and women who leave their personal stamp on history.

Now, the very concept of leadership implies the proposition that individuals can make a difference. This proposition has never been universally accepted. From classical times to the present day, eminent thinkers have regarded individuals as no more than the agents and pawns of larger forces, whether the gods and goddesses of the ancient world or, in the modern era, race, class, nation, the dialectic, the will of the people, the spirit of the times, history itself. Against such forces, the individual dwindles into insignificance.

So contends the thesis of historical determinism. Tolstoy's great novel *War and Peace* offers a famous statement of the case. Why, Tolstoy asked, did millions of men in the Napoleonic Wars, denying their human feelings and their common sense, move back and forth across Europe slaughtering their fellows? "The war," Tolstoy answered, "was bound to happen simply because it was bound to happen." All prior history determined it. As for leaders, they, Tolstoy said, "are but the labels that serve to give a name to an end and, like labels, they have the least possible connection with the event." The greater the leader, "the more conspicuous the inevitability and the predestination of every act he commits." The leader, said Tolstoy, is "the slave of history."

Determinism takes many forms. Marxism is the determinism of class. Nazism the determinism of race. But the idea of men and women as the slaves of history runs athwart the deepest human instincts. Rigid determinism abolishes the idea of human freedom—the assumption of free choice that underlies every move we make, every word we speak, every thought we think. It abolishes the idea of human responsibility, since it is manifestly unfair to reward or punish people for actions that are by definition beyond their control. No one can live consistently by any deterministic creed. The Marxist states prove this themselves by their extreme susceptibility to the cult of leadership.

More than that, history refutes the idea that individuals make no difference. In December 1931, a British politician crossing Fifth Avenue in New York City between 76th and 77th streets around 10:30 P.M. looked in the wrong direction and was knocked down by an automobile—a moment, he later recalled, of a man aghast, a world aglare: "I do not understand why I was not broken like an eggshell or squashed like a gooseberry." Fourteen months later an American politician, sitting in an open car in Miami, Florida, was fired on by an assassin; the man beside him was hit. Those who believe that individuals make no difference to history might well ponder whether the next two decades would have been the same had Mario Constasino's car killed Winston Churchill in 1931 and Giuseppe Zangara's bullet killed Franklin Roosevelt in 1933. Suppose, in addition, that Lenin had died of typhus in Siberia in 1895 and that Hitler had been killed on the western front in 1916. What would the twentieth century have looked like now?

For better or for worse, individuals do make a difference. "The notion that a people can run itself and its affairs anonymously," wrote the philosopher William James, "is now well known to be the silliest of absurdities. Mankind does nothing save through initiatives on the part of inventors, great or small, and imitation by the rest of us—these are the sole factors in human progress. Individuals of genius show the way, and set the patterns, which common people then adopt and follow."

Leadership, James suggests, means leadership in thought as well as in action. In the long run, leaders in thought may well make the greater difference to the world. "The ideas of economists and political philosophers, both when they are right and when they are wrong," wrote John Maynard Keynes, "are more powerful than is commonly understood. Indeed the world is ruled by little else. Practical men, who believe themselves to be quite exempt from any intellectual influences, are usually the slaves of some defunct economist.... The power of vested interests is vastly exaggerated compared with the gradual encroachment of ideas."

But, as Woodrow Wilson once said, "Those only are leaders of men, in the general eye, who lead in action. . . . It is at their hands that new thought gets its translation into the crude language of deeds." Leaders in thought often invent in solitude and obscurity, leaving to later generations the tasks of imitation. Leaders in action—the leaders portrayed in this series—have to be effective in their own time.

And they cannot be effective by themselves. They must act in response to the rhythms of their age. Their genius must be adapted, in a phrase from William James, "to the receptivities of the moment." Leaders are useless without followers. "There goes the mob," said the French politician, hearing a clamor in the streets. "I am their leader. I must follow them." Great leaders turn the inchoate emotions of the mob to purposes of their own. They seize on the opportunities of their time, the hopes, fears, frustrations, crises, potentialities. They succeed when events have prepared the way for them, when the community is awaiting to be aroused, when they can provide the clarifying and organizing ideas. Leadership completes the circuit between the individual and the mass and thereby alters history.

It may alter history for better or for worse. Leaders have been responsible for the most extravagant follies and most monstrous crimes that have beset suffering humanity. They have also been vital in such gains as humanity has made in individual freedom, religious and racial tolerance, social justice, and respect for human rights.

There is no sure way to tell in advance who is going to lead for good and who for evil. But a glance at the gallery of men and women in MODERN WORLD LEADERS suggests some useful tests.

One test is this: Do leaders lead by force or by persuasion? By command or by consent? Through most of history leadership was exercised by the divine right of authority. The duty of followers was to defer and to obey. "Theirs not to reason why/Theirs but to do and die." On occasion, as with the so-called enlightened despots of the eighteenth century in Europe, absolutist leadership was animated by humane purposes. More often, absolutism nourished the passion for domination, land, gold, and conquest and resulted in tyranny.

The great revolution of modern times has been the revolution of equality. "Perhaps no form of government," wrote the British historian James Bryce in his study of the United States, *The American Commonwealth*, "needs great leaders so much as democracy." The idea that all people should be equal in their legal condition has undermined the old structure of authority, hierarchy, and deference. The revolution of equality has had two contrary effects on the nature of leadership. For equality, as Alexis de Tocqueville pointed out in his great study *Democracy in America*, might mean equality in servitude as well as equality in freedom.

"I know of only two methods of establishing equality in the political world," Tocqueville wrote. "Rights must be given to every citizen, or none at all to anyone . . . save one, who is the master of all." There was no middle ground "between the sovereignty of all and the absolute power of one man." In his astonishing prediction of twentieth-century totalitarian dictatorship, Tocqueville explained how the revolution of equality could lead to the *Führerprinzip* and more terrible absolutism than the world had ever known.

But when rights are given to every citizen and the sovereignty of all is established, the problem of leadership takes a new form, becomes more exacting than ever before. It is easy to issue commands and enforce them by the rope and the stake, the concentration camp and the *gulag*. It is much harder to use argument and achievement to overcome opposition and win consent. The Founding Fathers of the United States understood the difficulty. They believed that history had given them the opportunity to decide, as Alexander Hamilton wrote in the first Federalist Paper, whether men are indeed capable of basing government on "reflection and choice, or whether they are forever destined to depend . . . on accident and force."

Government by reflection and choice called for a new style of leadership and a new quality of followership. It required leaders to be responsive to popular concerns, and it required followers to be active and informed participants in the process. Democracy does not eliminate emotion from politics; sometimes it fosters demagoguery; but it is confident that, as the greatest of democratic leaders put it, you cannot fool all of the people all of the time. It measures leadership by results and retires those who overreach or falter or fail.

It is true that in the long run despots are measured by results too. But they can postpone the day of judgment, sometimes indefinitely, and in the meantime they can do infinite harm. It is also true that democracy is no guarantee of virtue and intelligence in government, for the voice of the people is not necessarily the voice of God. But democracy, by assuring the right of opposition, offers built-in resistance to the evils inherent in absolutism. As the theologian Reinhold Niebuhr summed it up, "Man's capacity for justice makes democracy possible, but man's inclination to justice makes democracy necessary."

A second test for leadership is the end for which power is sought. When leaders have as their goal the supremacy of a master race or the promotion of totalitarian revolution or the acquisition and exploitation of colonies or the protection of greed and privilege or the preservation of personal power, it is likely that their leadership will do little to advance the cause of humanity. When their goal is the abolition of slavery, the liberation of women, the enlargement of opportunity for the poor and powerless, the extension of equal rights to racial minorities, the defense of the freedoms of expression and opposition, it is likely that their leadership will increase the sum of human liberty and welfare.

Leaders have done great harm to the world. They have also conferred great benefits. You will find both sorts in this series. Even "good" leaders must be regarded with a certain wariness. Leaders are not demigods; they put on their trousers one leg after another just like ordinary mortals. No leader is infallible, and every leader needs to be reminded of this at regular intervals. Irreverence irritates leaders but is their salvation. Unquestioning submission corrupts leaders and demeans followers. Making a cult of a leader is always a mistake. Fortunately hero worship generates its own antidote. "Every hero," said Emerson, "becomes a bore at last."

The single benefit the great leaders confer is to embolden the rest of us to live according to our own best selves, to be active, insistent, and resolute in affirming our own sense of things. For great leaders attest to the reality of human freedom against the supposed inevitabilities of history. And they attest to the wisdom and power that may lie within the most unlikely of us, which is why Abraham Lincoln remains the supreme example of great leadership. A great leader, said Emerson, exhibits new possibilities to all humanity. "We feed on genius. . . . Great men exist that there may be greater men."

Great leaders, in short, justify themselves by emancipating and empowering their followers. So humanity struggles to master its destiny, remembering with Alexis de Tocqueville: "It is true that around every man a fatal circle is traced beyond which he cannot pass; but within the wide verge of that circle he is powerful and free; as it is with man, so with communities." ●

CHAPTER

1

War and a Young Boy Named Ban Ki-moon

FROM 1939 TO 1945, THE WORLD WAS AT WAR. A NUMBER OF NATIONS divided into the Axis Powers and the Allies were fighting for much of the world's fate. During this time, in a small village on the Korean Peninsula—then occupied by Japan—a baby boy was born; his name was Ban Ki-moon. After the war, the child's country earned its independence from Japan when Korea was divided into two nations with differing governments. South Korea's independence coincided with the creation and start of the United Nations. Fifty-one countries had joined together in hopes of making World War II the last war of its kind, forming an organization that would work for global peace and security.

On June 25, 1950, the effectiveness of the United Nations was put to the test when North Korea unexpectedly attacked its neighbor sharing the same peninsula, South Korea, with a force of 135,000 men. After some debate, the United Nations

After World War II ended, the Korean peninsula was split into two countries: North Korea and South Korea. Although both sides wished to unify the country, their different viewpoints about government soon led to war. When North Korea invaded South Korea, the newly formed United Nations was forced to send troops and delegates *(above)* to help restore peace and security between the two nations.

came to South Korea's aid, sending in forces in September of that year. During the war, which lasted until 1953, young Ban Ki-moon was forced to flee with his family from their village and home. For three years, they hid in a remote location while bombing and fighting continued all around them. As Ban grew to be a young man, he came to appreciate the support the United Nations had provided in helping to keep his nation from being overtaken.

Ban had an early connection with the UN, when in 1956, his class chose him to write a letter to then secretary-general

Dag Hammarskjöld regarding the Hungarian uprising against Russians. He was never sure if the UN leader ever read the letter, and as a matter of fact, he was not even certain his message had ever been sent. But it would be his first attempt to make a difference with the United Nations.

In high school, Ban traveled to the United States where he had the once-in-a-lifetime opportunity to meet President John F. Kennedy, a moment that sparked within him a desire to work for peace. The year before the South Korean high school student made that overseas trip, the United Nations had elected U Thant as its third secretary-general and first-ever Asian head of the world organization. As Ban moved into a diplomatic career, U Thant became another leader he would admire. Even before finishing his master's degree, Ban began serving in his nation's Foreign Ministry. For 37 years, he continued to work for the South Korean Foreign Ministry, serving 10 of those years on UN-related missions. He became known for his strong work ethic, his skill as an administrator, and his tact as a diplomat—especially during the Six-Party Talks with North Korea, held to prevent that nation's development of nuclear weapons. Eventually Ban's reputation earned him his position as South Korean foreign minister in 2004.

Two years later, in February 2006, when dealings with North Korea were still high on the United Nations' agenda, the South Korean government announced its nomination of Ban for the job of secretary-general, a vacancy that had to be filled when Kofi Annan stepped down at the end of December. In its official announcement of Ban's candidacy, the South Korean government said, "In the process of building the 11th-largest economy in the world upon the ruins of war, of surmounting authoritarian rule to realize democratization, we overcame many of the challenges in nation-building, development, and peace and security that the global community is faced with in many corners of the world today." When the seasoned diplomat won the election for the post, things had come full circle for both Ban and his native country.

Dag Hammarskjöld, a Swedish diplomat once described by President John F. Kennedy as "the greatest statesman of our century," served as the secretary-general of the UN during part of Ban's childhood years. As an elementary school student, Ban was chosen by his classmates to write a letter to Hammarskjöld regarding an international event in Eastern Europe.

The nation that had emerged from war would now have one of its own leading the organization that helped to save it decades earlier, and the boy who witnessed the events of those years was now the man in charge.

CHAPTER

2

The United Nations Begins

WORLD WAR II CAUSED DEVASTATION PREVIOUSLY UNKNOWN TO humankind: entire nations were left in ruins, millions died, and the Jewish population in Europe had been marked for extinction by Adolf Hitler's Holocaust. But from the dust and debris rose a world body—the collaboration of numerous nations—to maintain global peace and improve conditions for all humanity. This organization is the United Nations.

The United Nations is a well-recognized organization around the world, but it is not entirely unique. Since the dawn of civilization, global peace and security have been at stake and the lust for power found within humankind. Thus, other attempts at collaborative peacekeeping have occurred in world history.

THE INTERNATIONAL PEACE CONFERENCE

In 1899, by the initiation of Russia's emperor, the first International Peace Conference was held in the city of The

Hague in the Netherlands. The intention of this conference was to reduce the number of arms among the world's nations, determine ways to settle global crises by peaceful means, prevent future wars, and draw up rules of engagement for use during warfare. A second conference was held, again at the impetus of Russia's ruler, in the Netherlands in 1907. The two meetings failed to reduce armaments, but several of the declarations and conventions that resulted were ratified later by a number of nations, including guidelines for protecting noncombatants. One of the largest successes of the First Hague Conference was the founding of the Permanent Court of Arbitration, also called the Hague Tribunal, which began its work in 1902. Here, nations in dispute may agree to let the court hear their arguments and settle the issue at hand. In 1998, even with the development of the UN and its own judicial body, the Hague Tribunal had 88 countries that still adhered to its conventions. A third peace conference was scheduled to convene in 1916. This meeting, however, had to be canceled because of the start of World War I.

THE LEAGUE OF NATIONS

Decades before the UN would emerge to keep peace around the globe, circumstances similar to those that resulted in its creation were happening in the world. In 1914, the world stage was shook by a war that erupted in Europe. America's president at the time, Woodrow Wilson, held a firm belief that the United States should remain neutral in these affairs, working as a mediator and not as a combatant. That neutrality, however, would not last. On May 17, 1915, a German U-boat sunk the *Lusitania*, a large ocean liner filled with passengers. Almost 2,000 people, including 114 Americans, became casualties of war. The incident stoked anger in the American public, and President Wilson—while still demanding an apology from the German nation—tried to maintain his neutral stance. Conditions on the seas and around the globe worsened, and by April 2, 1917, Wilson was compelled to ask Congress to make a formal

When World War I ended, President Woodrow Wilson *(above)* hoped to avoid future conflict by establishing a coalition of countries dedicated to maintaining world peace. Known as the League of Nations, the group disbanded shortly after World War II, but served as a precursor to the United Nations.

declaration of war. The conflict remained in full force until the war's end on November 11, 1918.

Earlier that year, on January 8, Wilson addressed Congress with his Fourteen Points speech. The fourteenth point called for a world body that Wilson hoped would result in a lasting peace for all of the world's nations. The point read: "A general association of nations must be formed under specific covenants for the purpose of affording mutual guarantees of political independence and territorial integrity to great and small states alike."

After the war, Wilson took part in the Paris Peace Conference, which was held in 1919. There, he desperately tried to have his fourteen points adopted as part of the treaty ratified at the conference. Although these points did not make their way into the Treaty of Versailles, Wilson did succeed in having provisions for the creation of a League of Nations added into the final agreement. Ironically, because of political wrangling, the United States never joined the organization that had been developed to promote international cooperation and to work for peace and security. Because the League of Nations was unable to achieve its goals of maintaining global harmony and was unable to stop the worldwide conflict that resulted in World War II, the group disbanded in 1946. The League of Nations, however, was not forgotten, and much of its structure and many of its goals were incorporated into the formation of the United Nations that came later.

A NEW WORLD BODY

In 1945, after the atrocities and destruction of World War II, which ended officially with Japan's surrender on September 2 of that year, the representatives of 50 different nations converged on San Francisco to take part in the United Nations Conference on International Organization. This meeting ultimately resulted in the UN that exists today. The UN, however, was not born in one day or even one conference; discussions and meetings occurred among various heads of state long before the conference in San Francisco that June.

The Declaration of St. James's Palace (The London Declaration)

By 1941, the Axis Powers of Germany, Italy, and Japan had been wreaking havoc around the globe for two years. By June,

"IT IS OUR INTENTION TO WORK TOGETHER, AND WITH OTHER FREE PEOPLES, BOTH IN WAR AND PEACE, TO THIS END."

–The Declaration of St. James's Palace

London was home to a total of nine exiled governments and was itself the scene of bomb hits and air raids; almost all of the European continent had fallen to the Axis Powers.

Knowing further action had to be taken, a group of representatives from the countries of Australia, Canada, Great Britain, New Zealand, and the Union of South Africa, as well as the nine exiled governments—Belgium, Czechoslovakia, France, Greece, Luxembourg, the Netherlands, Norway, Poland, and Yugoslavia—met together at London's St. James's Palace. Here, at this ancient site, they signed a declaration, hoping for peace. Words from the declaration of June 12 read: "The only true basis of enduring peace is the willing cooperation of free peoples in a world which, relieved of the menace of aggression, all may enjoy economic and social security; it is our intention to work together, and with other free peoples, both in war and peace, to this end."

The Atlantic Charter

Two months after the London Declaration was signed, the Axis Powers were still going strong, and the war had yet to see the entrance of the United States. Although the United States was not officially engaged in war at the time, it did not stop President Franklin D. Roosevelt from a meeting at an undisclosed location on the high seas with British prime minister Winston Churchill. The charter they developed, neither a treaty nor a legally binding document, was intended to promote peace and a better future for the world and provide hope for those currently occupied nations. Created on August 14, 1941, it outlined issues such as not changing territorial boundaries without the consent of the peoples affected, the right of a nation to choose its own government, and the necessity for countries to have equal access to raw materials. This joint declaration by the two world leaders also called for nations to work collectively with regard to economics in order to improve labor standards and economic advancement around the globe. The Atlantic Charter, as it came to be known, was met with support upon Churchill's return to London and was signed by the USSR and the nine occupied nations that had also signed the London Declaration.

Two of the charter's eight points necessitated a world organization, with the eighth point stating, "They believe that all of the nations of the world, for realistic as well as spiritual reasons, must come to the abandonment of the use of force. Since no future peace can be maintained if land, sea, or air armaments continue to be employed by nations which threaten, or may threaten, aggression outside of their frontiers, they believe, pending the establishment of a wider and permanent system of general security, that the disarmament of such nations is essential. They will likewise aid and encourage all other practicable measures which will lighten for peace-loving peoples the crushing burden of armaments."

The United Nations Declaration

The next step leading to the United Nations' development came on New Year's Day in 1942, when Roosevelt, Churchill, Soviet diplomat Maxim Litvinov, and Chinese official T.V. Soong all signed a brief document, which later became known as the United Nations Declaration because of the use of the phrase "declaration by United Nations" by Franklin Roosevelt in the document's text. The very next day, January 2, representatives of 22 additional countries showed their support and signed

Meeting for the first time during World War II, President Franklin D. Roosevelt *(left)* and British Prime Minister Winston Churchill *(right)* devised the Atlantic Charter. This charter was not a treaty or an agreement, but a statement of mutual goals both leaders wished to achieve in the upcoming years. One of those goals was the formation of an international organization where countries would work together to prevent future conflict.

the document. By signing, all 26 nations were pledging their governments to the maximum war effort in fighting the Axis Powers and an agreement not to make separate peace accords.

The United Nations Charter

The four governments that had originally drawn up the United Nations Declaration met again and worked between August and October of 1944 to come up with separate proposals for the shaping of the new world body. All nations who had subscribed to the United Nations Declaration by March 1945 and who had declared war on Germany and Japan were invited to the conference set to take place in San Francisco that June. When the 50 countries met, they deliberated on the proposals submitted by China, the Soviet Union, Great Britain, and the United States. On June 26, 1945, representatives of all 50 nations signed the United Nations Charter. Poland, which was not in attendance at the conference, signed later and became one of the original UN member states. The UN's official start date, and the date United Nations Day is celebrated every year, was not until a few months later, on October 24, 1945, when the charter was ratified by China, France, the Soviet Union, the United Kingdom, the United States, and a majority of the other original 50 signatories. The UN's original 51 member states include Argentina, Australia, Belarus, Belgium, Bolivia, Brazil, Canada, Chile, China, Colombia, Costa Rica, Cuba, Czechoslovakia, Denmark, Dominican Republic, Ecuador, Egypt, El Salvador, Ethiopia, France, Greece, Guatemala, Haiti, Honduras, India, Iran, Iraq, Lebanon, Liberia, Luxembourg, Mexico, Netherlands, New Zealand, Nicaragua, Norway, Panama, Paraguay, Peru, Philippines, Poland, Saudi Arabia, South Africa, Syrian Arab Republic, Turkey, Ukraine, Union of Soviet Socialist Republics, United Kingdom of Great Britain and Northern Ireland, United States of America, Uruguay, Venezuela, and Yugoslavia.

The UN Charter itself aims to uphold human rights and suggests that its nations work together to fight social, economic, humanitarian, and cultural issues. Its preamble states

> WE THE PEOPLES OF THE UNITED NATIONS DETERMINED
>
> to save succeeding generations from the scourge of war, which twice in our lifetime has brought untold sorrow to mankind, and

> to reaffirm faith in fundamental human rights, in the dignity and worth of the human person, in the equal rights of men and women and of nations large and small, and
>
> to establish conditions under which justice and respect for the obligations arising from treaties and other sources of international law can be maintained, and
>
> to promote social progress and better standards of life in larger freedom,
>
> AND FOR THESE ENDS
>
> to practice tolerance and live together in peace with one another as good neighbours, and
>
> to unite our strength to maintain international peace and security, and
>
> to ensure, by the acceptance of principles and the institution of methods, that armed force shall not be used, save in the common interest, and
>
> to employ international machinery for the promotion of the economic and social advancement of all peoples,
>
> HAVE RESOLVED TO COMBINE OUR EFFORTS TO ACCOMPLISH THESE AIMS
>
> Accordingly, our respective Governments, through representatives assembled in the city of San Francisco, who have exhibited their full powers found to be in good and due form, have agreed to the present Charter of the United Nations and do hereby establish an international organization to be known as the United Nations.

UN HEADQUARTERS

The first meetings of the UN occurred in numerous places. The General Assembly session in 1946 was divided into two parts, held in London in February and in Flushing, New York, from October to December. The first 24 meetings of the Security Council were held in London, as was the first session of the Economic and Social Council that occurred on February 23, 1946. The Trusteeship Council did not have

ON DECEMBER 10, 1945, THE U.S. CONGRESS MADE A UNANIMOUS DECISION TO INVITE THE ORGANIZATION TO LOCATE ITS MAIN SITE IN THE UNITED STATES.

its first meeting until 1947, when members gathered at Lake Success, New York. With meetings occurring at all these various sites, it soon became obvious that a permanent, international headquarters was necessary to accommodate the many meetings to be held as well as the numerous representatives of member states. Until the new headquarters could be built, most UN bodies met in the interim in the New York locations of Hunter College, the Henry Hudson Hotel, and Lake Success.

Many countries vied for and were suggested as locations for the organization's permanent international headquarters site. On December 10, 1945, the U.S. Congress made a unanimous decision to invite the organization to locate its main site in the United States. After debating on the variety of places suggested, the UN's first General Assembly agreed on February 14, 1946, to select the United States to host its headquarters. Various cities within the United States were considered for the site—Philadelphia, Boston, San Francisco—but once an offer came in from millionaire John D. Rockefeller Jr., for the UN to purchase a parcel of land on New York City's Manhattan Island at the price of $8.5 million, UN members in the General Assembly decided it was an offer they could not refuse. The area, which then was a run-down section of town complete with slaughterhouses, industrial buildings, and a railroad barge landing, became the home office for dignitaries from around the world.

The creation of the United Nations involved the drafting and signing of the UN Charter, a document stating the goals of the organization. In 1945, fifty countries met in San Francisco *(above)* to consider proposals for the charter, which was ratified several months later.

CONSTRUCTION BEGINS

Construction of the UN's four main buildings began on October 24, 1949—United Nations Day—under the purview of the lead architect, Wallace K. Harrison of the United States. Assisting him in the development were 10 additional design professionals representing nations from across the globe, including Australia, Belgium, Brazil, Canada, China, France, the Soviet Union, Sweden, the United Kingdom, and Uruguay. The same day that construction began, a dedication ceremony took place in which the UN's first secretary-general, Trygve Halvdan Lie, laid the cornerstone while U.S. president Harry S. Truman looked on. The cornerstone itself was inscribed with the words "United Nations" in the five official languages used at that time—Chinese, English, French, Spanish, and Russian—as well as Roman numerals indicating the date the stone was laid. Inside the cornerstone, which rests underground to the east of the library building on the UN site's southern boundary, a metal box was placed that contains a copy of the UN Charter and the Universal Declaration of Human Rights, as well as a copy of the schedule of meetings and a variety of other documents, such as meeting records.

The result of the construction was four main buildings that all sit overlooking New York's East River: one for the Secretariat, which is the tallest at 39 above-ground stories (and three below ground), one for the General Assembly, one for a conference area that includes council chambers, and one for a library.

A SMALL CITY

The UN's official postal address is United Nations, New York, New York 10017. The land on which it sits, however, is not United States territory. The site is owned by the United Nations, and thus it is considered international territory. That means no U.S. official or officer, whether federal, state, or local can enter United Nations grounds or buildings without the express permission of the UN secretary-general. This policy stands for even police officers or military personnel. The UN, however, does have an agreement with its host country, the United States, not to harbor any person or persons wanted by U.S. authorities and seeking to avoid arrest.

Sitting on 18 acres, the UN headquarters, which even has its own team of firefighters and post office branch, sees hundreds of thousands of people through its doors each year. The delegations that represent all 192 member states send approximately 5,000 people to the New York site each year for the General Assembly sessions that take place. An additional staff of almost 5,000 people who work for the Secretariat call the UN offices home. At any given time, the number of journalists covering the UN and its issues of concern can range from 3,600 to 10,000. Visitors are welcome to tour the UN, and they do so in droves, to the tune of about 700,000 curious sightseers every year.

CHAPTER

3

The UN and Its Work

A TOTAL OF 6 BILLION PEOPLE RESIDE ON OUR EARTH, AND THE DELEGATES of the United Nations represent them all. The UN carries out its important work of keeping international peace and security and encouraging friendly relationships among countries through a system of six main bodies and various agencies, funds, and programs.

THE GENERAL ASSEMBLY

The General Assembly is the UN's main forum for debate when considering the most pressing problems affecting the world's peoples. Every year, from September to December or during special or emergency sessions, the General Assembly meets to discuss and work toward resolution of any subject covered under the UN Charter; such topics may range from issues of international security to the UN budget. In 2004, the General Assembly dealt with 150 separate topics. Each

ANY DECLARATION THE BODY CHOOSES TO MAKE SHOWS A COUNTRY THE WORLD'S OPINION ON AN ISSUE AND REFLECTS THE MORAL AUTHORITY OF A COMMUNITY OF NATIONS.

annual meeting begins with all member-state representatives providing a statement on their view of current world events in a general debate.

Here, unlike any other body within the UN, each of the 192 member states receives one vote when deciding issues. For key decisions, such as those related to international peace and security, the addition of new members, or the organization's budget, a two-thirds vote is required. When other matters are under consideration, a simple majority vote is all that is needed for approval. A recent development within the General Assembly, however, is to bring about consensus, rather than take a formal vote.

If a decision or declaration is made that involves a particular nation, the UN General Assembly cannot force that state to take any action it may recommend. However, any declaration the body chooses to make shows a country the world's opinion on an issue and reflects the moral authority of a community of nations.

THE SECURITY COUNCIL

The UN Charter provides for a Security Council within the UN to ensure peace and security around the world. This UN body has 15 members: 5 permanent members—China, France, Russia, the United Kingdom, and the United States—as well as 10 temporary members that rotate every two years. The council president changes each month according to the English alphabetical order of the member states.

When international disputes arise, the UN Security Council *(above)* is often called upon to help settle them. While the council often recommends peaceful means for settling conflicts, it also has the power to recommend economic sanctions, suspension from UN privileges, and the deployment of UN peacekeeping forces.

Meetings of the Security Council can take place anytime peace is under threat. Gatherings are sometimes held in places other than the New York headquarters, such as in 1972, when a session was convened in Addis Ababa, Ethiopia, and in 1973, when a session was held in Panama City, Panama. Unlike the General Assembly, however, which meets intermittently, the Security Council functions year round, with representatives of each member nation on-site at UN headquarters at all times. Whereas the General Assembly does not have the power to enforce its declarations, the Security Council can take action to bolster its decisions toward peace.

For any decision to pass in the council, unless the vote involves only procedural matters, nine yes votes are required. In addition, a decision can be blocked by a single no vote from any one of the five permanent members. Whenever a threat to international security arises, the council first considers any and all peaceful solutions, such as mediation between the parties involved. When mediation is undertaken, a special representative or the secretary-general him- or herself may be appointed to outline principles to settle the issue at hand peacefully. If actual fighting is taking place, the goal is to end it as quickly as possible by garnering a cease-fire agreement.

To enforce its decisions, the Security Council can take such actions as imposing economic sanctions and arms embargoes and, very rarely, authorizing the use of military force. According to the UN Charter, member states must follow any council decision. The Security Council is also responsible for sending out various UN peacekeeping missions meant to maintain truces, keep opposing forces apart while peaceful settlements are sought, and reduce overall tension in troubled areas. As of 2007, the UN had 15 active peacekeeping missions comprised of 100,000 troops across the globe in areas such as Haiti, Liberia, the Middle East, and Kosovo. In some nations, UN forces have been stationed for decades, such as the 59 years they have been active in Lebanon and Syria and in Pakistan and India, and 43 years in Cyprus.

THE ECONOMIC AND SOCIAL COUNCIL

To work toward solving issues of international economics, social ills, and health crises, as well as encourage cultural and educational cooperation among nations and promote human rights, the UN has the Economic and Social Council (ECOSOC). Just as its name indicates, this group handles all matters economic, social, humanitarian, and cultural in nature. The body, which has 54 members elected by the General Assembly, partakes in activities as varied as conducting studies and issuing reports regarding these topics to overseeing commissions on human rights, population growth, technology, or drug trafficking. It may also choose to assist in the preparation of any international conference related to economic and social issues.

The ECOSOC's responsibility is massive and includes coordinating the work of 14 UN specialized agencies, 10 functional commissions, and 5 regional commissions, as well as reports from 11 different UN funds and programs. The group's task is so large that it utilizes 70 percent of the UN's total resources—both human and financial.

THE INTERNATIONAL COURT OF JUSTICE

The UN's main judicial branch is the International Court of Justice, or World Court, located not at the organization's New York headquarters, but rather at the Peace Palace in the The Hague, Netherlands. It is the only one of the UN's six major bodies with headquarters outside of the United States. The official languages of the court are English and French.

This UN division began its work in April 1946, and within it are 15 judges elected for nine-year terms by both the General Assembly and the Security Council. Administrative tasks of the court are covered by a staff called the Registry. The judges preside over legal disputes brought to the court by different nations, basing their decisions on international law. The judges also provide opinions and make advisements on legal matters regarding any of the other main UN bodies or the organization's specialized agencies.

Decisions of the court are binding, but a few times within its over 60-year history, nations have refused to accept its rulings. Some of the court's recent decisions include a ruling in 2006 against Argentina, which attempted to suspend paper mill projects in Uruguay, and a 2005 ruling that Uganda must

The International Court of Justice *(above)*, located in The Hague, is responsible for settling international legal disputes between countries and also provides legal opinions for the UN General Assembly. The court bases its decisions on existing treaties and common practices and principles in the major legal systems around the world.

compensate the Democratic Republic of the Congo for looting that occurred during the war from 1998 to 2003. In 2004, the court ordered that the convictions of 51 Mexicans sitting on death row in the United States must be reviewed.

THE SECRETARIAT

Responsible for the day-to-day operation and work of the UN is the Secretariat, which consists of 9,000 staff members from 170 different countries. Approximately 5,000 work in the offices of the New York headquarters, while the remaining employees are scattered in other locations around the world. The UN Secretariat has an especially large presence in the cities of Addis Ababa, Ethiopia; Bangkok, Thailand; Beirut, Lebanon; Geneva, Switzerland; Nairobi, Kenya; Santiago, Chile; and Vienna, Austria. At the head of this vast staff and overseeing all of the Secretariat's activities is the UN's secretary-general.

The work of the Secretariat includes the administrative tasks needed to carry out the UN programs and policies devised by the organization's other bodies. Its duties are quite varied and depend on the current issues faced by the organization. The Secretariat may be required to administer peacekeeping forces to troubled areas, survey economic trends, or prepare studies regarding human rights. It also reports to the world media on the UN's diverse activities. Other services handled by staff of the Secretariat include the organization of international conferences and the interpretation of speeches and translation of papers into the UN's official languages.

THE TRUSTEESHIP COUNCIL

The last of the six main UN bodies, the Trusteeship Council, actually suspended its activities on November 1, 1994. Its job was to promote the political, economic, social, and educational advancement of the UN's Trust Territories and work toward these territories achieving self-governance or complete independence. The council was so successful in its work that all of the territories either became separate states themselves or joined neighboring, independent nations. The Trusteeship Council ended its work one month after the last of its Trustee Territories, Palau, located in the South Pacific, gained its independence. The council, which is made up of the same five members of the Security Council—China, France, Russia, the United Kingdom, and the United States—agreed that it would meet again should the need arise.

THE UN SYSTEM

In addition to the six main bodies of the UN, the organization is comprised of a system that includes 14 independent agencies and a large number of programs and other agencies of the UN's own. Among the independent agencies are the World Bank and the World Health Organization (WHO). The World Bank offers loans, financial advice, and other economic-related resources to more than 100 developing countries. In the area of health is the WHO, which provides leadership in global health matters such as monitoring disease outbreaks and assessing the performance of health systems around the world.

Examples of the UN's own major agencies are the World Food Programme (WFP) and the International Atomic Energy Agency (IAEA). The WFP exists as the UN's main agency to carry on the fight against hunger in nations around the world. The IAEA acts as the world's center of cooperation in the nuclear field. Other agencies within the system are involved in such varied activities as working to protect the environment, working to reduce poverty, setting standards for air travel, and providing aid to refugees.

UN MEMBERSHIP

Currently, the UN has 192 members, almost all of which have permanent missions at the New York headquarters. The first nations added to the ranks of the original 51 members were Afghanistan, Iceland, Sweden, and Thailand, which all joined in 1946. The most recent nation to join the world body was Montenegro in 2006. Previous to that, Switzerland and Timor-Leste became new members in 2002. In 2000, the UN membership grew to 189 nations, with the addition of the Federal Republic of Yugoslavia and Tuvalu. A flux of new states joined the UN upon the breakup of the Soviet Union in the early 1990s.

In order to be admitted to the UN, a nation must be recommended by the Security Council and then receive a two-thirds majority vote in the General Assembly. Members of the UN contribute to the cost of running the organization. Each nation is evaluated individually to determine its ability to contribute. At present, the largest UN contributor is the United States, which in 2006 provided over $5.3 billion to the UN system.

WHAT THE UN HAS DONE

In its 60-plus-year history, the UN has succeeded in many ways. The following are just some of the actions the world organization has taken to help maintain global peace and to make the world a better place to live.

Human Rights

The UN has put forth a great deal of effort to promote human rights around the globe, having developed over 80 conventions and treaties on the topic. Its most well-known accomplishment in this area, however, may be the Universal Declaration of Human Rights proclaimed by the General Assembly in 1948. This declaration outlines what should be the basic rights of all human beings: life, liberty, and nationality; free thought, conscience, and religion; the right to work and be educated; the right to food and housing; and the right to participate in government. In the area of human rights, the UN is now trying to move from setting standards such as these to the actual passing of human-rights laws.

International Law

Another aspect of the UN's work is the creation of international law. One example is the Kyoto Protocol, which went into effect on February 16, 2005, as an effort to prevent further global warming by reducing greenhouse gases emitted from nations around the globe. The Kyoto Protocol was ratified by a total of 140 countries.

United Nations Messengers of Peace

In 1997, Secretary-General Kofi Annan created the United Nations Messengers of Peace program in which widely recognized individuals in such fields as the arts, entertainment, and sports, volunteer to help bring global attention to the UN, its goals, and its work. Annan enlisted the help of nine such volunteers. As a token of appreciation for their service, each peace messenger receives a framed citation and an exclusive dove pin meant to symbolize peace. These high-profile messengers included world heavyweight boxing champion Muhammad Ali; international tennis ace from India, Vijay Amritraj; Italian author and journalist Anna Cataldi; American actor Michael Douglas; chimpanzee research pioneer Jane Goodall; Algerian-born singer and composer Enrico Macias; acclaimed jazz musician Wynton Marsalis; beloved opera singer Luciano Pavarotti; writer and Nobel Peace Prize winner Elie Wiesel; and renowned cellist Yo-Yo Ma.

After several months in office as secretary-general, Ban Ki-moon announced on September 21, 2007, some additions and deletions to the roster of international peace messengers. Added were conductor Daniel Barenboim, Brazilian author Paulo Coelho, Japanese-American violinist Midori Goto, and Olympic equestrian Princess Haya of Jordan. Gone from the list were Ali, Marsalis, Amritraj, Macias, and Cataldi. In addition to making these announcements, Ban paid tribute to Pavarotti, messenger of peace for nearly 10 years, who died earlier that month, on September 6. Of the famous tenor Ban said his "heart was even bigger than his voice."

International Day of Peace

In 1981, the General Assembly proclaimed that on the opening day of its regular session every year, an International Day of

The International Day of Peace, a day of remembrance and hope, is celebrated each year on September 21. Created in 1981, peace day has been a successful way to promote peace and unity throughout the world. *Above*, former UN secretary-general Kofi Annan rings the Peace Bell in 2005.

Peace should be celebrated to honor and strengthen ideals for peace among all the world's nations. The peace day now occurs on the same date each year, September 21. The UN marks the special day with a ceremony near the UN Peace Bell. This bell, located on the front lawn of the Secretariat building and made from coins contributed by the people of 60 different countries, was a gift to the UN from the United Nations Association of Japan. First, the secretary-general gives a special message and then rings the bell, asking people everywhere to take a moment of silence to think about the goal of world peace. After this portion of the ceremony, the president of the Security Council offers a statement on behalf of its members.

Outside the UN, it is hoped that others will honor the moment of silence. On this day, many civic organizations and school groups plan events and ceremonies of their own. For individuals to commemorate the day, the UN suggests activities such as organizing a peace walk, planting a tree, or visiting a nursing home or hospital.

Other Accomplishments

The list of the UN's triumphs and successes is indeed long and varied. A few more examples provide a glimpse of the UN's wide-ranging effect on the world's peoples. In Europe and North America, the amount of acid rain falling has been reduced thanks to several UN environmental conventions. Each year, with about $30 billion in aid, the World Bank, the UN Development Programme, and other agencies help less-developed nations. In 2003, the World Food Programme set a record during its then 40 years of service by providing food to 110 million people. That same year, the UN helped raise $3.4 billion to aid victims of war and natural disasters, and because of the World Health Organization's global efforts, the devastating disease of smallpox has been eradicated from the globe.

CHAPTER

4

Who Is Ban Ki-moon?

BAN KI-MOON GREW UP IN A TIME OF WAR. IN THE KOREAN WAR, WHICH pitted north against south, UN forces came to South Korea's aid. This conflict and the UN's help turned out to have a profound influence on what Ban would go on to do later in life—namely become an internationally known and greatly respected diplomat.

SOUTH KOREA

The country of South Korea can be found in eastern Asia near the Sea of Japan and the Yellow Sea. In an area just slightly larger than the state of Indiana resides a population of almost 50 million people. Overall, the country's climate is temperate, with more rain falling in summer than winter, but because of its location typhoons sometimes strike the nation. Much of the land is hilly, with numerous mountains; to the west and south, however, plains dominate. The Asian nation is made up of nine

> "We [South Koreans] wish to become the strongest advocate of the agendas of the United Nations, be it peace, development or human rights."
>
> —Ban Ki-moon

provinces and claims seven metropolitan cities, including its capital, Seoul.

KOREA UNITES—ONLY TO SEPARATE

As long ago as the seventh century, three separate states joined together to form one independent nation—Korea—a union that lasted into the twentieth century. Like the history of most nations, South Korea's is unique, and part of its unique history is how much the country was affected by war. Immediately following the Russo-Japanese War that started in 1904 and ended in 1905, the Korean Peninsula became a protectorate governed by Japan. Five years later, in 1910, the country then became a Japanese colony. World War II brought even more change when the Japanese surrendered to the United States in 1945. It was then that the one nation was divided in two—the Democratic People's Republic of Korea in the north with its communist-style government, and the Republic of Korea in the south. More war was to follow, with the South fighting off attacks from the North in the Korean War, which started in 1950. The war ended in 1953 with an armistice agreement signed by the two opposing sides that resulted in the 2.5-mile-wide (4 kilometer) Demilitarized Zone at the 38th parallel.

In May 2006, Ban included a comment about the effects of war on South Korea in an address to the UN Council on Foreign Relations, "Confidence in the face of adversity comes naturally to Koreans. We Koreans have quite literally risen from the ashes of this war. We have done so through hard work, commitment, dedication and the help of friends, and particularly the United Nations. Now we stand ready to pay back what we owed to the United Nations and international community. We wish to become the strongest advocate of the agendas of the United Nations, be it peace, development or human rights."

SOUTH KOREA PROSPERS

Although South Korea remained under military rule for 32 years, it worked its way toward democracy with its first civilian president, Kim Young-sam, in 1993. Dr. Arne Kislenko, a professor of history and international relations, emphasized this point by saying to a reporter after Ban's election as secretary-general, "The government of South Korea has really changed in many ways and it's really shaken the image of a largely militaristic state. Ban is kind of an illustration of that, very progressive, very western-educated." The nation, which became an official UN member state in 1991, has experienced tremendous economic growth over the years. Forty years ago, South Korea's economy could easily have been compared with the poorer countries of today's Africa, but in 2004, the nation's economy moved into the trillion-dollar territory.

THE YOUNG KOREAN

Ban Ki-moon, the self-declared "farm boy," was born on June 13, 1944, in the rural village of Eumseong in the North Chungcheong province of Korea. At the time, this area was occupied by Japan. Because of the heavy fighting of the Korean War, Ban and his family were forced to relocate to a remote mountainside where Ban says they were safe, but poor and hungry—and where as a young boy of only six, he could see the planes bombing nearby towns. Here, his family remained hidden from the fighting for three years. It was not until after the war that Ban encountered Americans for the first time. In an interview with a *New York Times* reporter Ban said, "After the war, the American soldiers would throw biscuits and chocolates and chewing gum to us, and all our clothes were given to us by America."

From first grade onward, Ban and his family made their home in Chungju, a town centrally located on the Korean Peninsula. It was here that he grew up as part of a middle-class family and the oldest of six children, until the unfortunate bankruptcy of his father's warehouse business.

BAN VISITS THE UNITED STATES

As a way of learning English in school, Ban and his schoolmates were required to write specific sentences in English a total of ten times to memorize them. Ban's hard work learning the language paid off in 1962, when at the age of 18, he won an English-language contest sponsored by the American Red Cross. The story of his win and his prize—a trip to the United States—made news in the local paper. A nearby girls' school decided to honor Ban with a traditional symbol of luck, a group of bamboo strainers. Little did Ban know that at the presentation given by the girls, he would meet his future wife and life partner, Yoo Soon-taek.

Ban's trip to the United States included an eight-day stay with a host family in San Francisco. Libba Patterson, the host family mother, remembered fondly the young South Korean on his first international excursion, saying that he was both mature and wise for his 18 years. When Ban made his first visit to San Francisco as secretary-general in July 2007, he made certain to stop in and see Patterson, with whom he has maintained a relationship for more than five decades. Ban even called her when he found out he was up for the chief UN position. During Ban's visit to the West Coast, Patterson recounted to reporters one funny moment from his stay all those years ago: "I had bought some rice and told him I can cook that up, but he said he wanted a hamburger."

That trip to the United States made another lasting impression on the young man, when he met then U.S. president John F. Kennedy. In a June 2007 interview with *Parade* magazine, Ban spoke of the president's influence on him: "I saw how he contributed to world peace and security."

Through a contest sponsored by the American Red Cross, Ban Ki-moon won a trip to the United States and a chance to meet President John F. Kennedy in 1962. Inspired by Kennedy's efforts to maintain world peace, Ban decided he would become a diplomat. *Above*, Ban, second from left, listens to Kennedy during a visit to the White House.

After finishing his bachelor of arts degree in international relations at Seoul National University in 1970, Ban went on to Harvard University in Cambridge, Massachusetts. There, in 1983 at the Kennedy School of Government, he showed his sense of humor when he introduced himself as J.F.K., or "Just from Korea." Ban finished at Harvard in 1985 with a master's degree in public administration.

THE BEGINNING OF A DIPLOMAT

Ban's service to his country began even before finishing his master's degree. In 1975, he had his first real experience with politics and his first connection with the United Nations by working as a civil servant in the South Korean Foreign Ministry's UN division. Ban continued to serve the Republic of Korea for 37 years in a string of important positions within the Foreign Ministry, including director-general for American Affairs (1990–1992), deputy minister for policy planning (1995), chief national security advisor to the president (1996), vice foreign minister (2000), foreign policy adviser to the president (2002), and foreign minister (2004–2006). The diplomat's driving goal throughout his work in the ministry was to maintain peace between both North Korea and South Korea and to spread that peace as much as possible throughout the world.

Ban's global postings included two terms as counselor at the Embassy of the Republic of Korea in Washington, D.C., acting as first secretary at the Republic of Korea's Permanent Mission to the UN in New York, and becoming director of the UN Division at the Foreign Ministry's Seoul headquarters. The diplomat's first post abroad was in New Delhi, India, where he garnered knowledge of development issues. Ban has said that in choosing his early postings, he selected those that would allow him to save money that he could send back home to his family.

BAN GAINS FAME

Ban became an international figure when he served overseas as the South Korean ambassador to Austria, a diplomatic role that lasted from 1998 to 2000. Austria is well known as a neutral country when it comes to global affairs. This led to Ban becoming chair of the Preparatory Commission for the Comprehensive Nuclear-Test-Ban Treaty Organization (CTBTO) during his ambassadorship. The CTBTO was established after the collapse of the Soviet Union. Ban took over as head of this body in 1999, a time when efforts were underway to raise the group's profile. At that time, the treaty itself was only three years old and had been signed by only a few nations. The South Korean used his diplomatic skills to muster support from other countries.

In this position, Ban made a memorable impression. Wolfgang Hoffman had been the CTBTO's executive secretary when Ban entered the picture. In an interview in November 2006 after Ban's selection as the UN's new secretary-general, Hoffman said, "He can be tough and knows his mind." In an interview around the same time, Ban's personal assistant at the CTBTO, Jo-Ann Koch, remarked on her boss's kindness and caring attitude, stating that he was the only official ever to show his gratitude for her work by thanking her with a gift.

THE RESPECT FOR BAN GROWS

Ban earned many accolades for his work after the terrorist attacks in the United States on September 11, 2001. The day after the attacks marked the start of South Korea's presidency of the UN, and Ban had stepped in as chef de cabinet of the incoming Korean General Assembly president. The quiet leader and capable administrator used his skills to promote a sense of cooperation and unity among the UN's member states, bringing order to the chaotic atmosphere that tumultuous week. Ban—responsible for facilitating the first UN resolution condemning the attacks—also oversaw changes in procedure that allowed the UN to take quicker action in times of crisis. As chef de cabinet, Ban handled the situation so well that three years later in 2004, he was appointed to the highly visible role of South Korean foreign minister.

As his nation's foreign minister, Ban made even further contributions to maintaining global peace and security. During his two-year, ten-month tenure as South Korea's top diplomat, Ban made visits to an impressive 111 countries and talked business with many of his foreign counterparts at an astounding 374 meetings.

PEACE AND NORTH KOREA

As both foreign minister and ambassador to the UN, Ban was heavily involved in the Six-Party Talks among China, Japan, North Korea, Russia, South Korea, and the United States to find a peaceful, diplomatic resolution to the world dispute over North Korea's development of nuclear weapons. The South Korean played a big part in bringing about the adoption of a joint statement on resolving the issue of nuclear weapons and North Korea in September 2005.

Ban showed his continued concern for the subject when he hosted Kofi Annan in May 2006. Foreign Minister Ban worked alongside Secretary-General Annan in pressing North Korea to give up its nuclear ambitions. The two men also made it clear that they did not approve of the Bush administration's additional emphasis on North Korea's human-rights violations and counterfeiting. Ban and Annan felt that the nuclear issue should be at the forefront of negotiations with North Korean leader Kim Jong Il.

There may have been more than just coincidence at play when Ban's appointment as head of the UN was announced less than one week after North Korea claimed to have tested a nuclear weapon. In an interview with Korean newspaper *Hankyoreh* shortly after his election to the post of secretary-general, Ban spoke of his commitment to resolve the nuclear issue with North Korea, saying that to move the issue forward he would appoint a politician or diplomat who would be respected internationally. In a farewell speech to his South Korean Foreign Ministry colleagues, Ban said of the subject, "With regard to resolving the North Korea nuclear issue and maintaining peace on the Korean peninsula, I plan to best utilize my authority as secretary-general and contribute to resolving the issue peacefully as soon as possible."

During his time as South Korea's foreign minister, Ban Ki-moon's diplomatic style was beneficial when dealing with issues regarding Iraq and North Korea. His calm approach to negotiations helped establish a nuclear disarmament agreement with North Korea. *Above*, Foreign Minister Ban Ki-moon *(right)* accompanies former South African president Nelson Mandela *(left)*.

The Six-Party Talks continued into Ban's term as UN chief, and important progress was made. In February 2007, an agreement with North Korea was finally reached. Kim Jong Il's regime agreed to close its nuclear reactor and thus stop the production of plutonium in Yongbyon. It also agreed to let in an international inspection team to verify that North Korea had followed through with its promise. In exchange for closing the reactor, North Korea would receive 50,000 metric tons of fuel oil. The reactor was shut down in July. In September

SOME CITIZENS CALLED FOR BAN'S RESIGNATION DURING THIS TIME.

2007, more discussions took place and further agreement was reached regarding North Korea's disclosure of all its nuclear programs and the shutdown of any other nuclear facilities in exchange for more fuel oil and economic aid.

SURVIVING A TIME OF CRISIS

Ban's time as foreign minister was not all smooth sailing. On Friday, June 18, 2004, the South Korean government announced a plan to send an additional 3,000 troops to northern Iraq in August to join the 600 military doctors and engineers already there. Only two days later, Al Jazeera, the Arabic-language television news network based in Qatar, broadcast a disturbing video it received. In the clip, a hostage, South Korean Kim Sun-il, was seen begging for his home government to pull out of Iraq and screaming in English, "I don't want to die." The kidnappers claimed to be a group led by Abu Musab al-Zarqawi, a Jordanian terrorist with a connection to Al Qaeda. Speaking in Arabic, they gave South Korea a 24-hour ultimatum: "Our message to the South Korean government and the Korean people: We first demand you withdraw your forces from our lands and not send more of your forces to this land. Otherwise, we will send to you the head of this Korean, and we will follow it by the heads of your other soldiers."

The nation's officials held an emergency meeting because of the incident. The following day, June 21, Deputy Foreign Minister Choi Young Jin announced publicly that South Korea would not alter its decision to send the force of 3,000 into Iraq. Kim Sun-il, who had been working in Iraq as a Korean translator, was later beheaded on video.

The incident caused an uproar in South Korea, since many people in the nation did not agree with the government's decision to send troops into Iraq. Some citizens called for Ban's resignation during this time. The situation was so bad that cab drivers in the capital even refused to pick up and transport any Foreign Ministry workers. Ban, however, kept calm and did his best to appease the people of his country. The foreign minister made assurances that he would take a long, hard look at the ministry, and he established a 24-hour hotline to be used by South Koreans working overseas who might be experiencing trouble. Ban's efforts seemed to work. The situation blew over, and he became a well-respected foreign minister in the eyes of most South Korean citizens.

Ban became one of the longest-serving ministers in his nation's history, resigning after almost three years in November 2006, only to prepare for his new role as UN secretary-general. In a good-bye speech to South Korean parliament members, Ban said of his election as the new UN chief, "This diplomatic triumph belongs to all South Koreans. The honor can never be mine alone."

THE PERSONAL LIFE OF A DIPLOMAT

Ban and Yoo Soon-taek were the same age when they met during their high school years. She was her high school's student council president. The two went on to marry nine years later, in 1971, one year after Ban passed his exam to become a diplomat. Of his marriage to Yoo Soon-taek, Ban told a *New York Sun* reporter in December 2006, "I've had 35 years of honeymoon."

The couple started their family in 1972 with the birth of a daughter, Seon-yong. Their oldest daughter now works for the Korea Foundation in Seoul, an organization with the goal of promoting Korea's image and reputation around the globe through a variety of academic and cultural exchange programs. Their second child was a son, Woo-hyun, who was born in 1974. Woo-hyun, in similar fashion to his father's academic pursuits, is working on a master's degree in

Ban Ki-moon *(right)* met his wife, Yoo Soon-taek *(left)*, when she handed him bamboo strainers for luck on his trip to the United States. Married in 1971, Yoo Soon-taek often travels with her husband to developing countries and is heavily involved with UNICEF, a UN organization dedicated to the welfare of children.

business administration at the University of California at Los Angeles. Ban and Yoo Soon-taek's youngest daughter, Hyun-hee, was born in 1976 and, like her father, works in a global organization as a field officer for the United Nations Children's Fund (UNICEF) in Nairobi, Kenya.

Perhaps because he is so dedicated to his work, little has been published in the English-speaking world on Ban's personal life and interests. In a British news article about Ban becoming secretary-general, a former colleague of his, Park Soogil, said that the South Korean liked reading and golf, but that "his main hobby is work." Ban himself confirmed the statement when he told a *New York Times* journalist, "When you ask about hobbies, that's a question I have difficulty answering. I regret, looking back at my life, that I have not been able to cultivate any extracurricular activities like playing tennis or soccer or football. The only sport I do is golf, but in the last three or four years, I have played less than 10 times." The South Korean diplomat has professed that he is a workaholic and feels a bit sorry for his family because of it. On occasion, however, Ban does find time to listen to classical music. In regard to his religious beliefs, he has described himself as a nondenominational Christian, which is common in South Korea, where the religious makeup of its population, according to a 1995 census, is about 26 percent Christian.

A MAN OF HONOR

The seasoned diplomat has received many national and international awards, medals, and other honors. His work and service have touched numerous nations around the world. Three times, in 1975, 1986, and 2006, Ban received his nation's Highest Order of Service Merit. In 2001, Austria honored him with the Grand Decoration of Honor for his contributions as envoy there. The following year, the Brazilian government gave him its Grand Cross of Rio Blanco, and in 2006, Peru bestowed upon him its highest honor for diplomatic service, the Gran Cruz del Sol (Great Cross of the Sun). Algeria, Hungary, and El Salvador are just a few of the other nations that have chosen to recognize the hard-working diplomat's many contributions with special awards and honors.

CHAPTER

5

The Job of Secretary-General

IT'S THE MOST IMPOSSIBLE JOB IN THE WORLD—THAT'S WHAT FORMER UN secretary-general Kofi Annan said of this high-profile position. But just what is a secretary-general, and what makes it such a difficult and demanding job?

THE WORLD'S REPRESENTATIVE

In the UN Charter, the secretary-general is described as the UN's "chief administrative officer" and can be entrusted with other functions by the Security Council, General Assembly, and other UN organs. In Article 99, the UN Charter also states that this person can "bring to the attention of the Security Council any matter which in his opinion may threaten the maintenance of international peace and security." Although not a very long description, the text implies the weight of any secretary-general's responsibility. In giving these instructions about the secretary-general's role, however, the charter gives no specifications as to the type of leader this person should be, how the candidate should be selected, or how long this person should serve the world's peoples.

A Variety of Roles

Over the years, the men who have served in the role have been the ones to define it. Some secretaries-general have been quite active, like Dag Hammarskjöld, and some have been more bureaucratic, like Kurt Waldheim. In essence, the secretary-general must play many different roles: diplomat, advocate, civil servant, and CEO. The secretary-general symbolizes the ideals of the UN and is the voice of the world's populations, especially those considered poor and vulnerable. In one sense, this leader is expected to be his or her own political force. The secretary-general must be an expert at walking fine lines. At times, in this leader's role of speaking and acting for peace, he or she may face challenges from member states whose interests are at stake. Yet, at the same time, he or she is expected to be somewhat of a servant to the UN. This is one of the situations in which the diplomatic role of the secretary-general is called to service. He or she must listen to the member states' concerns, yet work on behalf of peace and security—and this is, probably, the world diplomat's most vital role: keeping international disputes from arising.

The roles of the secretary-general are numerous and varied. There are the administrative duties; he or she oversees the staff of the UN Secretariat, whose executive office alone consists of 9,000 employees from approximately 170 nations.

As a human resources leader, the secretary-general must choose 50 undersecretaries to head different areas, such as the UNICEF and UNDP (United Nations Development Programme) funds. In these instances of hiring, the secretary-general must negotiate with both the Security Council and the General Assembly to fill these positions with varied and diverse representatives from the large number of nations.

THE SECRETARY-GENERAL USES THE NEUTRAL POSITION OF LEADER OF A GLOBAL ORGANIZATION TO PREVENT AND STOP CONFLICT AROUND THE WORLD.

As peacekeeper, the man or woman in this role is responsible for overseeing the many peacekeeping missions sent by the UN; this includes 80,000 military people and 15,000 civilians. At the time of Ban's nomination, there were 18 separate peacekeeping missions in progress.

Another aspect of being secretary-general is acting as the world's mediator. As part of what is referred to as his or her "good offices," the secretary-general uses the neutral position of leader of a global organization to prevent and stop conflict around the world. Good examples of this were the promotion of armistice between Israel and the Arab states by Secretary-General Dag Hammarskjöld, and Secretary-General Javier Pérez de Cuéllar's negotiation of the cease-fire that eventually brought an end to the Iraq-Iran War.

The day-to-day schedule of a secretary-general can be full from morning until night, given the remarkable number of duties that fall under his or her responsibility. The secretary-general attends sessions of UN bodies, consults with world leaders and high-level government officials, and travels throughout the globe in an effort to stay in touch with the world's peoples and the events taking place. Another duty of the secretary-general is to issue a yearly report on the UN's recent work and future priorities. The secretary-general also acts as chairman of the Administrative Committee on Coordination (ACC). This meeting, which occurs twice yearly, involves the executive heads of all UN funds, programs, and specialized agencies. The intention is to manage and coordinate the numerous branches that make up the complex UN system.

Ban Ki-moon *(above)* was sworn in as UN secretary-general in 2006. As secretary-general, Ban has pledged to tackle problems concerning climate change, human rights, nuclear disarmament, and internal problems within the UN itself.

Term of Office

Officially, there is no limit to the number of terms that a single person can serve as the UN's secretary-general. Having served two terms already, the UN's fourth secretary-general, Kurt Waldheim, was being considered for a third term; but five more years did not happen for him when China vetoed his nomination. No person has ever stayed in the role of secretary-general for more than two five-year terms.

THE PREVIOUS SECRETARIES-GENERAL

In general, the men who have been selected for this very public role have been career diplomats from small- to medium-sized countries considered to be politically neutral.

Trygve Halvdan Lie

Politics came a bit into play in the selection of Trygve Lie as the United Nations' first secretary-general. At this time in history, the Cold War was continuing to chill relations between the Soviet Union and the United States and its perceived allies. Therefore, someone from a neutral country was needed to fill the position. The Soviets were adamant that whomever was selected *not* be a North American, British, or French national. The result was Norwegian Trygve Halvdan Lie. Born on July 16, 1896, Lie was educated at Oslo University and received his law degree there in 1919. That same year, he began work as the assistant to the secretary of the Norwegian Labor Party. Throughout the following years, he held many other important roles in the Norwegian government, such as the minister of justice in the Labor Party government, a position he maintained from 1935 to 1939. In December 1940, he became Norway's acting foreign minister and was appointed the official foreign minister several months later, in February 1941.

He led the Norwegian delegation to the UN Conference on International Organization, which took place in San Francisco in April 1945. He also served as chairman of Commission III, which was responsible for drafting the provisions for the Security Council in the UN Charter. Lie was elected secretary-general on February 1, 1946, and during his second term in November 1952, he resigned his position. Lie continued to stay involved in politics and global issues. He died on December 30, 1968.

Dag Hammarskjöld

Beginning on April 10, 1953, until September 1961, the UN was headed by Secretary-General Dag Hammarskjöld. The son of Sweden's prime minister during World War I, Dag Hjalmar Agne Hammarskjöld was born on July 29, 1905, in Jonkoping, a town in south-central Sweden. In 1925, Hammarskjöld earned his BA in linguistics, literature, and history from Uppsala University. Following that, he worked toward a degree in economics and finished a bachelor of laws degree in 1930.

That year, he became Sweden's secretary of a governmental committee on unemployment, a role he served for four years. During this time, he earned his doctorate in economics from the University of Stockholm. He then became an assistant professor of political economics and held various government positions. In 1947, Hammarskjöld was appointed to the Foreign Office as undersecretary. In 1951 and 1952, he served as vice chairman of the Swedish Delegation to the sixth regular session of the UN General Assembly in Paris. In the 1952 to 1953 seventh General Assembly session, Hammarskjöld served as acting chairman.

During his term as secretary-general, he worked to maintain peace between Israel and the Arab states, organized the UN Emergency Force in 1956, brought about a peaceful solution to the dispute over the Suez Canal, and secured the release of 15 American flyers who had been detained by the People's Republic of China. His active tenure came to an abrupt and tragic end in September 1961, when his plane crashed during a peace mission in the Congo. He was awarded the Nobel Peace Prize posthumously that same year for his work to strengthen the United Nations.

U Thant

The UN's first Asian secretary-general was chosen after Dag Hammarskjöld was killed in the air crash of September 1961. U Thant went on to serve two terms, from November 3, 1961, to December 31, 1971. The UN's third secretary-general was born in Pantanaw, Burma (present-day Myanmar), on January 22, 1909. He attended Pantanaw's National High School and University College in Rangoon. Before work as a diplomat, U Thant was an education and information professional. He served as the National High School headmaster, the press director of the government of Burma, the nation's director of broadcasting, and secretary to the government of Burma in the Ministry of Information.

Starting in 1957, U Thant became Burma's permanent representative to the UN, with the rank of ambassador. He stayed in this role until his election as secretary-general. At the end of his second term, U Thant retired. He died two years later on November 25, 1974 at the age of 65 as the result of a long illness. During his lifetime, he had received a long list of honorary degrees from colleges and universities around the world.

Kurt Waldheim

Following U Thant as secretary-general was Kurt Waldheim, an Austrian born in Sankt Andra-Wordern, near Vienna, on December 21, 1918. A graduate of the Vienna Consular Academy, Waldheim studied at the University of Vienna and became a doctor of jurisprudence in 1944. He joined the Austrian diplomatic service shortly thereafter, in 1945. In 1955, he was appointed the permanent observer for Austria to the UN and later headed the Austrian Mission when the nation was admitted to the organization. From 1964 to 1968, Waldheim served as the permanent Austrian representative to the UN. During that time, he was chairman of the Committee on the Peaceful Uses of Outer Space, and in 1968, he was elected president of the First UN Conference on the Exploration of Peaceful

Uses of Outer Space. His term as secretary-general began on January 1, 1972. As secretary-general, Waldheim made it a practice to visit areas around the world of special concern. He died at age 88 on June 14, 2007, in Vienna.

Javier Pérez de Cuéllar

Born in Lima, Peru, on January 19, 1920, Javier Pérez de Cuéllar began his first term as secretary-general in 1982. His background included years as a lawyer and career diplomat, serving as ambassador of Peru to Switzerland, the Soviet Union, Poland, and Venezuela. He joined the Peruvian Ministry of Foreign Affairs in 1940 and was a member of the Peruvian delegation to the first session of the UN General Assembly in 1946. In 1971, Pérez de Cuéllar became the permanent representative of Peru to the UN and in 1979 became the undersecretary-general for Special Political Affairs. Even before becoming secretary-general, the Peruvian had helped the then current secretary-general by visiting Pakistan and Afghanistan in April and August of 1981 to continue negotiations that the secretary-general had started between the two nations. Pérez de Cuéllar has been decorated by 25 countries.

Boutros Boutros-Ghali

The UN's sixth secretary-general was an Egyptian with a PhD in international law; his name was Boutros Boutros-Ghali. After securing a bachelor of laws degree from Cairo University in 1946, Boutros-Ghali finished his PhD at Paris University in 1949. From the same institution, he also had diplomas in political science, economics, and public law. Boutros-Ghali's career started in international affairs; he was a diplomat, jurist, scholar, and author of more than 100 publications and articles. In October 1977, Boutros-Ghali became Egypt's minister of state for foreign affairs, a position he held for 13 years. In 1978, he played a significant role in the Camp David Accords between Egypt and Israel. After this, he headed the Egyptian delegations to the UN's General Assembly in 1979, 1982, and 1990. Beginning in May 1991, he acted as Egypt's deputy prime minister for foreign affairs. Then, in January 1992, he began his term as UN secretary-general. Over the years, Boutros-Ghali has received awards and honors from 24 countries.

Kofi Annan

Kofi Annan, Ban's predecessor, began his term as the seventh secretary-general on January 1, 1997. Born in Ghana in 1938, he acquired degrees at the University of Science and Technology in Kumasi, Ghana; Macalester College in St. Paul, Minnesota; the Institute of International Affairs in Geneva, Switzerland; and the Massachusetts Institute of Technology's Sloan School of Management in Boston, Massachusetts. He joined the UN system in 1962, working as an administration and budget officer with the World Health Organization in Geneva. He held a variety of positions in the UN before becoming its undersecretary-general for peacekeeping in 1993.

Among the highlights of Annan's ten years of service as secretary-general was his creation of the new post of deputy secretary-general to help handle a job that had been growing in size and scope over the previous 60 years. Annan had a strong desire to modernize the UN and make the organization more effective. At his urging, the member states established two new bodies in the large organization: the Peacebuilding Commission and the Human Rights Council. He also developed a report looking at realistic ways to reduce political trouble and violence within and between African states. In January 1999, Annan proposed a global compact as a way for the UN to work with world businesses and help people around the globe share in the benefits of the global economy and marketplace.

In 2001, Annan—along with the UN organization—received the Nobel Peace Prize.

During their time in office, each UN secretary-general has dealt with major international incidents like the Arab-Israeli War, revolutions and emerging independent nations, nuclear disarmament, and genocide. *(Clockwise from top left)* Trygvie Lie, Dag Hammarskjöld, U Thant, Boutros Boutros-Ghali, Javier Pérez de Cuéllar, and Kurt Waldheim.

CHOOSING A SECRETARY-GENERAL

For most of the UN's 60-plus-year history, the general public, and even individuals inside the UN itself, have been somewhat baffled by the process of selecting a new secretary-general. What is known is that the 5 permanent and 10 elected members of the Security Council recommend one person to the

General Assembly for the role of secretary-general. What many insiders—and outsiders—find confusing are the unwritten rituals and traditions that the Security Council seems to follow in ultimately narrowing the field of candidates to a single individual. Allan Rock, an ambassador from Canada, studied the nomination process and called it "opaque, ill-defined, unpredictable, and unsatisfactory." Vaira Vike-Freiberga, candidate for the UN's eighth secretary-general, herself asked for more transparency in the nomination process.

Ban was fortunate to be a part of a selection process that was more open than any of those held previously. This time around, the Security Council publicly announced the formal candidates. In the past, these names, for the most part, had been kept secret—so secret in fact that one story says that Dag Hammarskjöld did not even know he was a candidate until he was told he won the nomination on April 1, 1953. Because of the secrecy and the date of the announcement, Hammarskjöld at first thought his win was an April Fools' joke.

The Security Council's single candidate emerges from multiple discussions—some heated—and informal voting sessions called straw polls. It is during these polls that the five permanent members of the Security Council, also known as the Permanent Five, maintain the right to veto candidates. As a result, any candidate not finding favor with one of these represented nations—Britain, China, France, Russia, and the United States—can eventually be eliminated from the process.

The straw polls work in a fairly simple manner. Those voting have to decide on one of three votes for each person in the running. Voting members receive ballots in the form of cards with three different possible boxes to check. Their choices include: encourage, discourage, and no opinion. These unofficial straw polls take place numerous times, but they do not necessarily provide a good idea of who will eventually win the nomination. Members sometimes change their minds about candidates, and someone who first received a "discourage" vote may later receive an "encourage" vote. The result can be that a candidate first considered a favorite may lose his or her standing as the front-runner in the next round of voting. The opposite can hold true as well, as was the case with Kofi Annan. In the informal voting that took place before his election, France had consistently vetoed him. The nation changed its vote at the last minute, and a man who had been constantly vetoed by one of the Permanent Five later secured the position as secretary-general.

The candidate to receive the Security Council's backing is the one who receives the most votes and no vetoes. Traditionally, the General Assembly has accepted the Security Council's final candidate.

ELECTING THE UNITED NATIONS' EIGHTH SECRETARY-GENERAL

By the time its search for the eighth secretary-general came about, the United Nations was 60 years old and now had 192 member nations in its General Assembly.

A handful of skilled individuals were officially nominated along with Ban Ki-moon for the Security Council's consideration.

The Nominees

The first public candidate nominated by his home country was Surakiart Sathirathai of Thailand. Sathirathai was deputy prime minister of the nation at the time of his nomination, but during the Security Council's process of selecting a single candidate, his government was overthrown. Sathirathai did, however, have the official support of the Association of Southeast Asian Nations, a group of ten Asian countries.

The second nomination was that of Jayantha Dhanapala. He had functioned as secretary-general of the Secretariat for Coordinating the Peace Process during 2004 and 2005, and was a former UN undersecretary for disarmament. He was nominated for the position of secretary-general by his nation of Sri Lanka.

Ban's nomination by his home country of South Korea was third and came in February 2006. In a question-and-answer session with AsiaSource Interview on September 26, 2006, Ban discussed his qualifications for leading the world body: "During 40 years of public service, I have spent almost 10 years relating to the work of the United Nations, starting from the staff of the United Nations division in the South Korean Foreign Ministry. Most recently I served as Chef de Cabinet to the President of the 56th Session of the General Assembly. During that time I was able to gain first-hand experience in mediating several different agendas among many different countries. These will be useful and valuable assets for me in discharging my duties as Secretary-General should I be elected."

The other candidates included Ashraf Ghani, nominated by Afghanistan. He had been that country's finance minister, as well as an adviser to the UN and on World Bank projects in China, India, and Russia.

Prince Zeid Ra'ad Zeid al-Hussein, nominated by Jordan, was the UN ambassador from that nation.

Shashi Tharoor, from India, was—like Ban—a career diplomat, serving and representing his country for almost 30 years.

Because no woman had ever served as secretary-general, a group called Equality Now launched a campaign to try to get qualified females recognized and nominated. Partly because of this campaign, Latvian president Vaira Vike-Freiberga was nominated by the countries of Estonia, Latvia, and Lithuania. She had spent over a year as Secretary-General Kofi Annan's special envoy for UN reforms. No Asian women were nominated, however, and that would prove to make the election of a female to the office of secretary-general a remote possibility.

The Importance of Asia

Most of the candidates for the UN's eighth secretary-general were Asian. The reason behind this is that among the unwritten traditions of selecting a new secretary-general, there is a regional rotation. Various world regions are given their turn to have someone representing their part of the world in this important leadership position. This tradition was not met without criticism, however. John Bolton, the U.S. ambassador to the UN, felt this longtime aspect of the process for selecting a secretary-general did not necessarily result in nominating the best person for the job. He believed the job should go to the person best qualified at the time—regardless of nationality—and voiced his opinion to the fact.

Bolton's criticism did not seem to phase the traditional process. Wide speculation during this election determined that it was almost a certainty that this would be Asia's turn. For one reason, there had not been an Asian in the position since U Thant of Burma ended his term more than 30 years earlier in 1971. Another important aspect was timing and the current state of Asia's importance in world affairs. Asia was a dynamic region; of the UN's members, the Asian group of nations was largest with 54 (followed by Africa with 53).

Ban's Nomination: To Support Him or Not to Support Him?

People speculated that the United States favored candidates Vaira Vike-Freiberga, president of Latvia, or former Afghani finance minister Ashraf Ghani, but both received vetoes by other members of the Permanent Five. Some saw the reluctance of the United States to support a diplomat from South Korea as stemming from South Korea's growing relations with China and the United States' disagreement with how Seoul was handling relations with North Korea.

On the other hand, the United States had made it clear that the new secretary-general must be someone on good terms with the United States, and Ban had strong ties to the country.

After working on major projects such as the UN's oil-for-food program with Iraq, Kofi Annan *(above)* was selected to serve as the seventh UN secretary–general. Hoping to strengthen the UN, he formed new initiatives, committees, and funds to help the organization cope with emerging issues that affect the world's peoples. While in office, Annan was also able to assist in issues involving transitioning governments and territorial disputes.

He had studied in America, had served in Washington two times as his nation's ambassador, and in Seoul had been head of the U.S. Department for the Ministry of Foreign Affairs. Although the United States might not agree with South Korea's handling of certain relationships, the nation does view the Asian country as an ally. U.S. support for Ban became much stronger after North Korean capital Pyongyang's underground test of an atomic weapon; the South Korean diplomat had experience dealing with North Korea on nuclear issues. Some people keeping track of the selection process also believed the United States wanted a capable manager in the secretary-general role because the UN system had grown so much over the years. Again, Ban fit the bill, since he was well respected as an efficient manager and administrator.

Ban's Critics

In the past, nominated candidates for secretary-general did not campaign for the position as presidential or congressional candidates might do in the United States. As a result, nationality, not agendas, were often more of a factor in the Security Council's final choice. This election process saw a difference, however. The candidates, Ban included, spoke at a variety of UN meetings and forums to secure backing for their candidacies. At first, Ban's campaign did not make much of an impression, and he later told one audience they should not confuse his modesty with indecisiveness.

This inability to make a splash with his campaign—in general, Ban's low profile—was part of what brought critics out of the woodwork once he became a front-runner for the job. Concerns arose in the press about how the seemingly soft-spoken diplomat would fare as head of the UN. One of the major criticisms was that people saw him as "soft" and docile and wondered if he could be assertive and contrary enough when dealing with governments opposing the UN. Even Ban knew that he had this image problem to contend with. In speaking

BUT EVEN CRITICS COULD NOT ARGUE BAN'S DETERMINATION AND STAMINA. HE WAS WELL KNOWN FOR A TOUGH WORK ETHIC THAT INVOLVED DIVIDING HIS DAILY WORK SCHEDULE INTO FIVE-MINUTE INCREMENTS THAT ALLOWED HIM TO FIT AS MUCH BUSINESS AS POSSIBLE INTO EACH DAY.

with news organization Agence France-Presse, Ban said, "I may look soft from the outside but I have inner strength when it's really necessary. I've always been very decisive. In Asian countries humility is regarded as a virtue. Soft-speaking should in no way be regarded as a lack of leadership or commitment."

Even in his home nation, Ban had his critics. These people, even friends, had taken to calling the diplomat Ban-jusa or Ban-chusa, a nickname that referred to the seasoned diplomat as merely a meticulous, low-ranking official or simple administrative clerk. But even critics could not argue Ban's determination and stamina. He was well known for a tough work ethic that involved dividing his daily work schedule into five-minute increments that allowed him to fit as much business as possible into each day.

Other worries from critics included speculation that the South Korean diplomat might be too willing to compromise in tough situations or try too hard to please people in charge. Other detractors believed that Ban's agenda was not explicit enough. They saw his campaign on UN reform, transportation, and the free market as vague and without much specific detail.

Most of the criticism, however, was in regard to the South Korean being too low-profile and not charismatic enough for this extremely public role, but that criticism may have well worked to Ban's advantage. Over the years, UN experts have commented that people too well known and with specific agendas are not usually deemed by member nations to be suited to the job of secretary-general. One UN expert in particular commented that in this race, the Permanent Five, especially the United States, probably did not want someone too strong, assertive, or aggressive. Instead, they wanted someone they could work with, what one source referred to as a "modest" secretary-general.

Ban's Supporters

For as many criticisms that might have come Ban's way, an equal or greater number of comments on his strengths and abilities also appeared in the press. He was described as a resolute man with a strong view and strong motivation who was not known for making enemies, but for making friends. In one interview, Ko Ki-Seok, a South Korean Foreign Ministry spokesperson said, "Minister Ban is a kind of iron-hand-in-the-velvet-glove person at work." Ko also commented on the care Ban had for his staff.

Others spoke of Ban's energy and ability to listen and get along well with others. Analysts agreed that this eighth secretary-general would need to be a harmonizer. Many people spoke out on Ban's ability to get along with all sides while building consensus in the process; he was known for bringing opposing parties to compromise. As reported in the *Times Online*, one diplomat in Seoul had this to say: "I think he has the capacity to do the Secretary General's job. He's a very able man. Ban is generally regarded as a very good troubleshooter, very good at compromises and building consensus. People who work with him say he's a good manager. He also has a good knowledge of the United Nations and people in New York have a very positive impression of him."

Park Soogil, another diplomat from Seoul who had worked with Ban, said the perception of Ban as weak was misleading. In an interview reported in the *Guardian*, Park had this to say: "In the Oriental culture leadership is assessed in a different way. One can look very affable, very gentle, but inside his mind he has a strong conviction…appearance is one thing, his firm beliefs and readiness to make tough decisions is another." Park concluded by saying that Ban knew "how to disagree without being disagreeable."

Former U.S. ambassador and current president of the United Nations Association of the USA William H. Luers described Ban as an impressive candidate who knew his stuff, someone who was very thorough when speaking about important issues. Luers also commented that Ban had the necessary credentials as an experienced diplomat, the primary responsibility of a secretary-general.

The Straw Polls and Success

Ban led the Security Council's first two straw polls, on July 24 and September 14, but the road to his nomination would not be won that easily. On September 28, he suffered a setback, and in a new secret ballot, the diplomat received only 13 positive responses from the council's 15 members. Somewhere along the way, Ban had lost a vote, but he was still ahead of the other six candidates. In his favor, however, Ban would have fewer candidates to compete against; the day following these results, Jayantha Dhanapala withdrew from the race. On October 2, the Security Council held what would be its last straw poll. After the vote, China's permanent representative to the UN said, "It is quite clear from today's straw poll that Minister Ban Ki-moon is the candidate that the Security Council will recommend to the General Assembly." As a result of the poll, Shashi Tharoor—the closest of the remaining candidates to Ban's first place, with 10 favorable votes and 3 unfavorable votes, including one veto—withdrew his candidacy.

Winning votes from both the United States and China was a crucial step for Ban. Often, the two nations do not see eye to eye, and Ban's acceptance by both of them was a coup. On October 4, Zeid Ra'ad Zeid al-Hussein and Ashraf Ghani withdrew their names, and Surakiart Sathirathai and Vaira Vike-Freiberga quickly followed, announcing the very next day that they would end their runs. Ban was the last person standing.

The Security Council's vote took place on October 9, resulting in its official nomination of Ban to the members of the General Assembly, who then elected him the UN's eighth secretary-general on October 13. He was the first Asian in more than 30 years to hold the position.

One might think that Ban's nomination would be a time of celebration for the diplomat. His selection, however, came on the heels of a well-publicized and shocking nuclear test by North Korea. While in Seoul, Ban told journalists at a press conference on October 9, "This should be a moment of joy. But instead, I stand here with a very heavy heart. Despite the concerted warning from the international community, North Korea has gone ahead with a nuclear test." The issue became one of many Ban would have to face in his five-year term.

CHAPTER

6

Ban Takes Control

THE NEW SOUTH KOREAN SECRETARY-GENERAL WAS INDEED SET TO TAKE on one of the most difficult jobs in the world. He was now to lead an incredibly vast and far-reaching organization. As an example of that vastness, he would have more than 100 special UN representatives stationed around the world. The new UN chief would have to remember a lot of names, not to mention the specifics of each individual's job. But Ban seemed ready and more than willing to take on this enormous responsibility.

BEFORE TAKING OFFICE

Even before Ban had officially begun his term, he was working hard to set the tone and agenda for his time as secretary-general. On December 8, 2006, at the UN's Correspondents Association Ball, the South Korean showed his sense of humor and received a wide round of applause when he said, "Allow me to introduce myself. My name is Ban. Not James Ban. I am not code-named 007, but I will take my office in '07." The secretary-general-to-be also took it upon himself to change the words to "Santa Clause Is Coming to Town" by singing, "Ban Ki-moon is coming to town."

Shortly before Christmas, Ban paid a visit to a place he would soon be spending a lot of time in—his new office on the thirty-eighth floor of the UN headquarters in New York. He was given an introduction to what his days might be like by Alicia Bárcena Ibarra, Kofi Annan's chef de cabinet. Ban was surprised to learn from Bárcena that the UN's first meetings of the day usually began at 9 A.M. Well known for his reputation as a hard worker, he questioned why they didn't start at 8 A.M. instead.

While most people in the United States spend December 31 reveling with anticipation to welcome the New Year at midnight, the situation at a certain New York hotel was a bit more subdued. At his hotel room and temporary home, Ban met with his transition team after dinner to prepare for the following day, which would be his first as UN secretary-general.

A MOVING DELAY

The UN sets aside an official residence for its leader, and most secretaries-general have been able to move their families into it right away. However, the 85-year-old townhouse at Sutton Place overlooking New York's East River was undergoing much-needed renovations when Ban began his term. This five-story, 14,000-square-foot home was receiving an overhaul for the first time since 1950. The UN General Assembly approved $4.9 million to fix up the place. Altogether, the townhouse repairs were scheduled to take about nine months and would include necessary work on the heating, cooling, plumbing, kitchen, and security. Among the specific repairs required were sealing plumbing leaks, renovating an elevator that was no longer safe, and replacing the old kitchen exhaust system, which was now a possible fire hazard. Until Ban's new family home was ready, he and Yoo Soon-taek lived at the exclusive Waldorf-Astoria hotel in New York.

FIRST DAY ON THE JOB AT NEW YORK HEADQUARTERS

The new secretary-general's first day onsite at his UN headquarters office occurred right after the New Year holiday, Tuesday, January 2, 2007. Ban was greeted at the UN by the honor guard. He then proceeded to the meditation chapel, a small room in the General Assembly building whose focal point is a huge block of iron ore that is dimly lit from above. Here, Ban stopped to honor those who had died while on UN peacekeeping missions. He then spent the day meeting with staff (including a closed meeting about dealing with recent criticism of the world body), sitting for his official portrait, and even carrying his tray and eating lunch in the UN cafeteria.

Another task the new UN chief took care of was announcing two of his crucial staff member selections. As his chief of staff he appointed Vijay Nambiar, a veteran Indian diplomat with former postings at the UN and in Pakistan, China, Malaysia, and Afghanistan, as well as a position as special adviser to Kofi Annan. As his spokesperson, Ban appointed Michéle Montas, a former award-winning radio broadcaster in Haiti who had personal experience with the strife happening in many places around the globe. The journalist came to the United States in 2003 after her husband, also a radio broadcaster, had been killed and the threats on her own life could no longer be ignored. Montas had UN experience, too, as a spokesperson for the General Assembly in 2004.

A CONTROVERSIAL FIRST DAY

Ban's term started with some controversy. The execution of former Iraqi leader Saddam Hussein had taken place at dawn on December 30, the weekend before Ban took office. Hussein had been hung in the exact location that many Iraqis had been killed while he was in charge. Ban said to reporters waiting

Although Ban Ki-moon's transition to his role as UN secretary-general was smooth, it was complicated by Saddam Hussein's execution, an event that sparked international controversy. *Above*, Ban shakes hands with a UN officer on his first official day as secretary-general.

outside the Security Council's doors, "Saddam Hussein was responsible for committing heinous crimes and unspeakable atrocities against the Iraqi people. We should never forget the victims of his crimes. The issue of capital punishment is for each and every member state to decide." The reason his comments caught attention was that the UN's traditional stance has been to oppose capital punishment on the grounds that it violates human rights. Ban's spokesperson, Montas, had to clarify the new secretary-general's statement by explaining that in his home country of South Korea, capital punishment is legal, and that UN policy had not changed; Ban had simply added his own nuance in addressing the subject. Only a few days later, Ban himself tried to allay the concerns raised by his original comment, saying at a news conference that he recognized the trend happening around the world in which the death penalty was increasingly being phased out.

YOO SOON-TAEK JOINS IN

As wife of the new secretary-general, Yoo Soon-taek found herself involved in UN activities as well. On January 23, 2007, the wives of other diplomats held a luncheon in her honor. At the event, she spoke of how she met her husband right after the first Asian secretary-general, U Thant, had been appointed and of Ban's admiration of the leader. To the women at the luncheon Yoo said, "Of course, he never imagined he'd follow in his footsteps, but I know he will try to inspire a new generation of young Asians to public service."

GOALS OF THE NEW LEADER

Ban did not take long to outline his top priorities as new head of the UN. The crisis in Darfur was among the list, and Ban began tackling it his first day at the New York headquarters. He promised immediate work on the crisis, including plans to meet the next day with his special envoy, Sweden's Jan Eliasson, with whom he had already begun discussions over the phone on New Year's Day. The new secretary-general also talked about plans to attend the African Union Summit set to take place at the end of the month in Addis Ababa, Ethiopia. There he intended to have a conversation with the Sudanese

"YOU COULD SAY THAT I'M A MAN ON A MISSION, AND MY MISSION COULD BE OPERATION RESTORE TRUST— TRUST IN THE ORGANIZATION AND TRUST BETWEEN MEMBER STATES AND THE SECRETARIAT."

—Ban Ki-moon

president as a way to engage himself in the diplomatic process and bring a peaceful resolution to the situation as quickly as possible.

Ban also identified making peace with North Korea as an important focus of his tenure. To reporters on his first day, however, he spoke out that he alone could not solve the ongoing issue: "Not a single person, including the secretary-general of the United Nations, not a single country, however strong, powerful, resourceful, cannot address [these issues]. We need to have some common effort." Ban spoke against simply using sanctions to punish North Korea's government and of the need instead to employ diplomatic efforts and talks with North Korea, committing himself to traveling to the heavily guarded nation whenever the need arose.

In an interview with the Al Jazeera television network, Ban said his first two priorities as secretary-general were to improve the efficiency of the UN Secretariat (to other press he commented that he would also like to repair the ties between the Secretariat and UN member states) and to promote discussion and negotiations with leaders in regions of conflict, such as the Middle East and Africa. In another area of UN reform, Ban had plans to modernize the organization's staff structure. UN reform was a prime issue for the South Korean, who told reporters at a press conference right after being sworn in, "You could say that I'm a man on a mission, and my mission could be Operation Restore Trust—trust in the organization and trust between member states and the Secretariat."

BAN'S FIRST INTERNATIONAL TRIP

As part of an important visit to the African continent and his first trip overseas as secretary-general, Ban spent some time in the Democratic Republic of the Congo, where he arrived at 1 A.M. on January 27 after a 14-hour plane ride from Paris. Darfur may have been a more publicized conflict, but here, too, human atrocities had been said to have taken place. A UN report on the numerous rapes, killings, and tortures stated that Congolese rebels were responsible for actually grilling humans on a spit over a fire, while other people were boiled alive in large vats of water or oil, and that even cannabalism had occurred. At the time of Ban's visit, the region had 18,000 UN peacekeepers in place—the largest deployment on the globe. As of February 3, 2007, 80 UN peacekeepers were among the many that had been killed.

Ban's first glimpse of the country reflected a completely different view, as he was greeted by many of its dignitaries and a red carpet. The rosy image did not last long, however: The diplomat took note of the terrible poverty all around (a person's average income is $700 per year; life expectancy is only 51 years) as the mile-long motorcade he was in drove through the night. Part of Ban's mission was to encourage those individuals living through the nation's hard times. Going on less than four hours of sleep, Ban spoke at the People's Palace and praised the Congolese people for their courage.

THE SECRETARY-GENERAL DAY TO DAY

The schedule Ban Ki-moon takes on as secretary-general can be grueling. As the head of the UN, Ban spends a lot of time abroad. Here is just one brief and particular example of how he spent a little over one week on the job.

Panama—June 2, 3, 4

Ban's schedule took him to Panama for three days, where he and his wife arrived on June 2, 2007. The secretary-general set

Ban Ki-moon's first trip as secretary-general was to the Democratic Republic of the Congo, a war-torn African country whose recent history includes a brutal dictatorship and horrific war crimes. While there, Ban praised the Congolese parliament for their efforts in maintaining a democracy, despite the hardships and challenges facing the country. *Above*, Ban *(left)* shakes hands with Congolese National Assembly president, Vital Kamerhe *(right)*.

out first thing the next morning, taking time to visit one of Panama's most important sites—the Panama Canal. The canal, which connects the Atlantic and Pacific oceans, allows passage for more than 14,000 ships annually. Ban received VIP treatment and was accompanied to the site by the nation's president, Martin Torrijos. The UN chief was given an opportunity most visitors are not offered—the chance to operate the canal's three sets of locks from within its control tower. Ban did this for a full hour, seeing two ships successfully through the intricate waterway.

After his time at the canal, the secretary-general stopped at Ciudad del Saber, the future home of an important United Nations central hub for the Latin American and Caribbean region. Ban also listened to a presentation on a study conducted by the Economic Commission on Latin America and the Caribbean, and the World Food Programme. Through this session, the UN leader learned how children's malnutrition in Central America and the Dominican Republic affects both the economy and society.

Following these events, Ban met with regional United Nations directors as well as other country staff members. In addition, he held a number of meetings with important officials. For example, he met with the secretary-general of the Organization of American States, Jose Miguel Insulza. The two talked about cooperation between the UN and the Organization of American States as well as democracy and economic growth in Latin America. The thirty-seventh session of the organization was beginning that evening with a theme on energy and sustainable development—development that works for the present without compromising possible future development—so the two leaders discussed this subject as well. Another top official Ban met with was Gert Rosenthal Koenigsberger, Guatemala's foreign minister. The topics of their conversation included criminal justice and Guatemala's border dispute with Belize. In a meeting with Panama's first lady, Vivian Fernandez de Torrijos, they discussed her work on behalf of the handicapped in her nation.

At the Organization of American States' General Assembly opening session that evening, Ban addressed the issues of global warming and climate change and specifically stressed that partnerships among nations were needed to fight the adverse effects global climate changes could cause.

Madrid, Spain—June 5, 6, 7

The next day, Ban left Panama and did not arrive at his next destination—Madrid, Spain—until the early morning of Tuesday, June 5. The secretary-general's schedule was as equally full here as it had been in Panama.

Ban's first order of business was a speaking engagement with the staff of the World Tourism Organization on the importance of tourism as a way of bringing different groups of people together. Later that afternoon, he met with officials such as the secretary-general of the Iberoamerican Cooperation, Enrique Iglesias, and with Àngels Mataró I Pau, the director-general of the United Nations Association in Spain. Ban's wife also played a role while abroad. She joined her husband for dinner that night at Zarzuela Palace with King Juan Carlos I and Queen Sofia.

Ban began his Wednesday by meeting with Spanish president José Luis Rodríguez Zapatero. Among the subjects the two men discussed were UN reform, climate change, Israeli-Palestinian relations, and Kosovo. The meeting was followed by a press conference.

More meetings with officials were on the agenda for the day, including one with Vice President María Teresa Fernández de la Vega, again on UN reform and climate change, but also on the under-representation of women within the UN at important decision-making levels.

The secretary-general then traveled outside of Madrid to visit the nearby city of Toledo. He returned for one more meeting with Don Juan Manuel Suárez Del Toro Rivero, the president of the International Federation of Red Cross and Red Crescent Societies. The next morning the UN chief and his delegation left Madrid for his next stop—Berlin, Germany.

Berlin, Germany—June 7, 8, 9

Ban arrived in Berlin Thursday morning, the day before the Group of Eight (G-8) summit, a meeting of the leading eight industrialized nations that occurs every year.

To get a jump start on the summit, Ban met individually with a number of leaders who had attended an early outreach session prior to the summit. Leaders he met with for serious talks included Indian prime minister Manmohan Singh; South African president Thabo Mbeki; Brazilian president Luiz Inácio Lula da Silva; and Mexican president Felipe Calderón. A topic of considerable discussion was climate change, and Ban made sure to point out that the technology and resources needed to cope with the issue are available but that the real need is political support.

Darfur was an important topic the secretary-general discussed with the chairperson of the Commission of the African Union, Alpha Oumar Konare. In particular, they talked about the joint United Nations–African Union force, the needs of the African Union forces, political negotiations, and the humanitarian crisis caused by the conflict.

Ban did not take the evening to rest; instead, he discussed the recent elections in Nigeria and the situation in the Niger Delta with the new Nigerian president, Umaru Yar'Adua. The secretary-general's last event of the long day was a dinner hosted by German foreign minister Frank-Walter Steinmeier.

The following day was filled with the G-8 summit and related activities in Heiligendamm, Germany. Here, at a press conference, Ban told reporters that it was appropriate for climate change to dominate discussions, as it is what he called "a defining issue of our era."

During a press conference in the heavily protected Green Zone of Baghdad, Iraq, Ban Ki-moon ducked behind a podium *(above)* when a mortar attack shook the building. Despite experiencing firsthand an attack on the safest area of Iraq, Ban did not retract his promise of sending more UN staff to the Middle Eastern country.

Taking advantage of every available moment and opportunity, Ban met with other world leaders when not involved in the summit's main sessions. Included were talks with Japan's prime minister, Shinzo Abe, regarding the main topic of climate change, as well as UN Security Council reform, Darfur, and the Six-Party Talks on North Korea; and with Italy's prime minister, Romano Prodi, on the situations in Afghanistan, Lebanon, and Somalia. The secretary-general's overseas trip ended on Saturday, June 9, when he departed for home and the UN headquarters in New York.

DANGER ON THE JOB

Any world leader is vulnerable to risk. A position of political prominence can put anyone in the line of danger, and early on that proved to be true for the mild-mannered secretary-general. Ban was attending a press conference in Iraq at the home of Prime Minister Nuri Kamal al-Maliki on March 22, 2007. The prime minister's home is located in Baghdad's Green Zone, an area of closed-off and heavily guarded streets in the city's center where U.S. occupation authorities live and work. During the discussion with reporters, a mortar attack hit nearby. When Ban heard the loud boom, he ducked. Windows shattered and plaster came down in flakes from the ceiling. A bodyguard tried to convince the prime minister to move to another, safer room, but al-Maliki merely brushed off the man's concern and asked him to go. Translators went on to translate Ban's last comment for those in the room, and then al-Maliki mentioned plans for a conference to take place in April. After making that announcement, the prime minister asked Ban if that was enough, to which the secretary-general replied yes. The two men left and the conference ended there.

Ironically, shortly before the attack, Ban had announced that he was considering adding more UN personnel in the area, since security in the war-torn nation had improved. The number of UN staff working in Iraq had been decreased purposefully after a tragic incident in 2003. In August of that year, a truck bomb exploded near the UN headquarters in Iraq, killing 22 staff members, including the chief UN representative in the country, Sergio Vieira de Mello.

The day following Ban's scare, the new secretary-general admitted to reporters that he was both surprised and shook up by the attack, saying that because of the blast, "I could see the wind and the dust inside the room, and it looked very dangerous." However, Ban went on to say that the incident would not keep him from following through with his plan to create a bigger UN presence in Iraq by placing more personnel there. The secretary-general refused to be deterred from his top priorities.

CHAPTER

7

Diplomat to the World

DURING HIS CAMPAIGN FOR THE ROLE OF UN SECRETARY-GENERAL AND UPON his election, Ban discussed several issues that would be among his top priorities. Among those were the crisis in Darfur, terrorism, the war in Iraq, climate change, and UN reform. Following are just some of the actions Ban took on these issues in his first year as leader of the UN.

DARFUR

Darfur is an arid and impoverished region located in the remote western part of Sudan. The region has been in turmoil since 2003. By September of 2007, at least 200,000 people had died, 2.2 million others had been displaced from their homes, and 4 million Darfurians were in need of humanitarian aid because of the fighting. The turmoil has limited aid workers in the region because of the surrounding danger, which includes killings, rapes, and pillaging. Sudan has not been the only nation affected by this crisis—fighting sometimes crosses over to nearby Chad and the Central African Republic as well. Located across Sudan's borders are various refugee camps for the millions who have been forced to leave their homes. The United States has called the situation in Darfur genocide.

Sudan's leader, President Omar al-Bashir, is not popular with the heads of many of the world's governments, namely because of his continued denial of human-rights abuses that have occurred while he has been in power. The Sudanese leader is also notorious for going back on his word. On November 16, 2006, however, after a meeting in Addis Ababa, Ethiopia, he agreed to let in peacekeepers, but only after extreme international pressure. According to the agreement, forces would be sent in through a three-phase approach. In phases one and two, the UN would provide backup to the existing African Union force involved in the conflict. Phase one was called the Light Support Package and would include about 200 personnel as well as material and equipment. Phase two was known as the Heavy Support Package and would consist of about 4,000 people who would help the African Union force in various capacities. In stage three, the most critical part of the agreement, a joint African Union–United Nations force of about 20,000 would be deployed. Al-Bashir specifically stated, however, that he wanted some say in the size of the force to be committed and in determining the chain of command. The Sudanese government was adamant about minimal UN influence and a stronger African representation in the troops, saying that a UN force alone would be equal to an invasion. Al-Bashir made his agreement to a UN mission formal via a letter to this effect sent to then secretary-general Kofi Annan on December 23, 2006. Annan had been leading diplomatic efforts at the time.

A Trip to Africa

At the end of January, not even a month into his new position as secretary-general, Ban went on his first international

Omar Hassan al-Bashir *(above, holding cane)*, president of the African nation of Sudan, has frustrated the UN with his demands and restrictions on their efforts to assist refugees in the country. Accused of orchestrating genocide in the Sudanese region of Darfur, al-Bashir has continued to obstruct the UN and African Union peacekeeping forces from protecting the victims of his dictatorship.

business excursion: a five-day trip to Africa, mainly to attend the African Union summit, where he intended to raise the issue of the continuing crisis in Darfur. On his way to the summit to be held in Addis Ababa, Ban told a reporter that he planned to appeal to Sudanese president al-Bashir to think about the millions of people suffering in his country and to stress that the leader could not let that suffering continue.

Among the UN chief's numerous meetings during that five-day trip, the one of special significance was that with the Sudanese president. For one hour on the fringe of the African Union summit meetings, Ban along with top officials, including the head of UN peacekeeping, Jean-Marie Guéhenno, sat and discussed with al-Bashir the tragic situation occurring in his country. Then for another 30 minutes, Ban met with the president for a one-on-one conversation. People who had been keeping a close watch on the crisis felt in the end that the meeting had gained little ground. UN officials had been anxious that the discussions between the secretary-general and al-Bashir would lead to movement on the issue, especially in regard to the deployment of a significant UN peacekeeping force.

Critics complained that the talks between the two leaders never went beyond discussions of the second phase. Ban himself, however, considered even this an accomplishment, stating that a secured agreement on phase two would help set in quicker motion the all-important third phase. The UN chief told a reporter that another crucial achievement was made in his hour and a half with the Sudanese leader: He had established trust with al-Bashir.

Ban had no intention of stopping there. He announced plans to send his own pair of negotiators to try to restart the process of needed political talks; this team consisted of the special envoy for Darfur, Jan Eliasson, and the special envoy for the African Union, Salim Ahmed Salim.

Progress

In April 2007, Ban had to ask President George W. Bush not to place more sanctions on the strife-torn country of Sudan because doing so would interfere with the secretary-general's ability to progress with more diplomatic approaches. Not long after, in June 2007, a hopeful sign toward resolution came when Sudan agreed to the specifics set forth by the Security Council in allowing UN peacekeepers into Darfur as part of a hybrid force.

Then on July 17, shortly after Ban completed a trip that took him to Afghanistan and Europe, where he purposely raised the Darfur issue, the secretary-general and the U.S. president met specifically to discuss the Darfur situation.

"I WANT TO SEE FOR MYSELF THE PLIGHT OF THOSE WE SEEK TO HELP, AND THE CONDITIONS UNDER WHICH OUR PEACEKEEPERS IN DARFUR WILL OPERATE."

—Ban Ki-moon

Progress was made. By a unanimous decision, the Security Council agreed to deploy up to 26,000 peacekeepers to the disturbed region at a cost of $2 billion for the first year alone. The resulting resolution included the okay to authorize use of force if needed to back the resolution, an option for the Security Council as explained in Chapter 7 of the UN Charter. Through resolution 1769, peacekeepers would have the right to use force to prevent attacks on themselves, to protect civilians and aid workers, and to support the implementation of a peace agreement.

At Sudan's insistence, the majority of peacekeepers were to come from surrounding African nations and would include the 7,000 currently overwhelmed troops who had been involved since 2003. Military personnel would account for up to 19,555 of those deployed, while the limit on civilian police officers was placed at 6,432. Once the full deployment of 26,000 is reached, the effort in Darfur will be the largest peacekeeping operation anywhere in the world. Ban said in a statement to the Security Council on July 31, 2007, "By authorizing the deployment of a hybrid operation for Darfur, you are sending a clear and powerful signal of your commitment to improve the lives of the people of the region, and close this tragic chapter in Sudan's history."

Ban Sees Darfur Up Close

The secretary-general took his first trip to Sudan on September 3, 2007. Part of his reason for the visit was to see the situation himself. At his arrival in Khartoum, the country's capital, the

UN chief told an audience, "I want to see for myself the plight of those we seek to help, and the conditions under which our peacekeepers in Darfur will operate."

That evening of his arrival in the African nation, Ban addressed the UN Association in Sudan. In his speech, he stated his reasons for the visit, specifically mentioning his goal to "lock in the progress we have made so far. To build on it so that this terrible trauma may one day end."

An article written by Ban, titled "What I Saw in Darfur," appeared in the September 14, 2007, edition of the *Washington Post.* In the piece, the secretary-general mentioned the many contributing causes to the region's crisis, including desertification, ecological degradation, and the scarcity of needed resources, especially water. He also discussed the situation's complexity.

In his week-long trip, Ban reported that he met with government officials as usual, but he also took time to meet with the people truly affected by the crisis—the villagers who have been forced to leave their own homes, the aid workers trying to support the people of Darfur, and the leaders of surrounding countries, such as Chad and Libya, where the situation is spilling over. In particular, Ban mentioned his visit just outside of northern Darfur's largest city, El Fasher. Here, he spent time at the El Salam camp, now temporary "home" to some 45,000 displaced from their true homes. Of the visit Ban said, "My heart went out to them. I felt their hopelessness and frustration." He said he was especially affected by the children he met and felt compelled to promise them that he would do his best to bring peace and to get them back home.

By this trip, Ban and al-Bashir had had three in-person meetings and several phone conversations since Ban had begun his duties in January. A UN official traveling with Ban had this to say in the *New York Times* about his boss's relationship with Sudan's president: "al-Bashir knows that the Secretary-General

An agreement between Sudanese president Omar Hassan al-Bashir and the combined peacekeeping forces of the UN and the African Union (AU) ensured that the troops in Sudan would primarily be African. Nigerian peacekeepers with the UN and the AU *(above)* prepare for a patrol outside a refugee camp in Darfur.

will be frank, but trusts him not to go parading around afterward saying, 'I told him a thing or two.'"

More Action on Darfur

Movement on Darfur now seemed to be coming at a faster pace than at any time in the conflict's four-year history. On September 21, 2007, Ban announced that a trust fund would be created to support the Darfur peace talks set to take place in Libya on October 27. In addition to including members of the Sudanese government, Ban said he would invite the eight major rebel groups at odds with the government to participate as well. The fund would be used to help facilitate and strengthen the diplomatic efforts needed to bring all involved parties to the table. The announcement came on the heels of a meeting cochaired by Ban and African Union Commission chairperson Alpha Oumar Konare, which occurred that same day at UN headquarters. During the meeting, which Ban called constructive, the representatives of 26 countries and regional groups—including Sudan—agreed to support the joint United Nations–African Union effort to help end the conflict.

The unanimous support was for a specific three-track approach to the situation: 1) achieving a political solution, 2) sending out a hybrid force of United Nations and African Union peacekeepers, which will be called UNAMID, and 3) providing civilians with humanitarian aid and help for recovery.

TERRORISM

Making good on his promise to make the somber subject of terrorism one of his top priorities if elected secretary-general, Ban—only a month and a half into office—announced a new tool for use as part of the already existing United Nations Global Counter-Terrorism Strategy adopted by the General Assembly the previous September. This strategy marked a first-ever agreement by the UN's 192 nations on how to take real, concrete actions to combat terrorism. Ban's offering to the fight was the *Counter-Terrorism Online Handbook*, which made its debut on February 16, 2007. In an introduction to the UN's member states on the *Handbook*, Ban said, "Together, we must demonstrate that we are up to the task. Whether we like it or not, our generation will go down in history as one that was challenged to protect the world from terrorism. We are challenged to do so by victims and survivors in New York, Bali, Nairobi, Riyadh, Bombay, Casablanca, Istanbul, Dar Es Salaam, Beslan, London and Madrid—where the trial of the 2004 bombings opened just yesterday, reminding us that the wounds of such an attack never fully heal. We are challenged to do so by the people of communities and countries whose economies and well-being are damaged by the impact of terrorism. We are challenged to do so by those who could become the vulnerable targets of the next attack. We cannot fail any of them. Let us unite in this mission."

The *Handbook* was developed by the Counter-Terrorism Implementation Task Force (CTITF), put together as part of the UN's Global Counter-Terrorism Strategy. The searchable online handbook provides member states, regional organizations, and United Nations country teams with a single, user-friendly source for information on the task force's activities and resources. It will allow quick and easy access to information on various assistance providers and facilitate faster contact with these providers.

As further example of his action on the subject, Ban led a meeting along with Afghanistan's president Hamid Karzai. The meeting focused on the opium and heroin production in Afghanistan that has been linked to the financing of terrorist activities. Gathered at the meeting were foreign ministers and diplomats from 18 different countries, some European, some Afghanistan's neighbors. Speaking to the press after the meeting, Ban said the group came to the conclusion that "breaking this linkage is vital to creating a stable, prosperous and democratic Afghanistan."

IRAQ

As the new secretary-general, Ban did not take long to begin addressing the war in Iraq either. He made a surprise, one-day visit to the war-torn country on March 22, 2007, at the beginning of a 10-day tour of the Middle East. While there, Ban spoke with Iraqi prime minister Nuri al-Maliki, and during their talks, Ban assured the prime minister of the UN's staunch commitment to help his nation's people. The secretary-general also spoke of the need to uphold human rights and the importance of all major political groups being included in the country's political process. Ban also met with UN staff working in the nation and took time to pay tribute to Sergio Vieira de Mello, the UN envoy killed with 21 others when the Iraq UN headquarters was bombed on August 19, 2003. To honor his memory, Ban laid a wreath at de Mello's monument.

On July 17, Ban met with U.S. president George W. Bush to discuss various issues, including the Iraq war. Only the day before, the secretary-general commented publicly for the first time on his thoughts of the ongoing debate in the United States regarding the pullout of its troops in Iraq. During a press conference in New York, Ban was asked about the UN's view of such a pullout; he had this to say in response: "It is not my place to inject myself into this discussion taking place between the American people and the administration and Congress. However, I would like to tell you that great caution should be taken for the sake of the Iraqi people. Any abrupt withdrawal or decision may lead to further deterioration of the situation in Iraq."

In August, the UN Security Council unanimously passed resolution 1770, which extended for another year the UN Assistance Mission in Iraq (UNAMI), which began in 2003. UNAMI's responsibilities, outlined by the new resolution, included assisting in political facilitation, national reconciliation, and promoting regional cooperation between Iraq and its neighboring countries. After the Security Council's meeting, Ban addressed reporters saying, "Promoting and encouraging political facilitation and dialogue among different factions and ethnic religious groups—this will be one of the important areas where the United Nations will be engaged."

Then in September, the UN chief met again with Iraq's Prime Minister al-Maliki as well as top officials from other countries in the region, the permanent members of the Security Council, and a variety of other high-level officials, including the foreign ministers of 20 different nations. These words were part of his opening remarks to the group of distinguished international representatives: "For the stability of Iraq, regional countries have an important role in securing their borders, confronting those who work to destabilize Iraq from within their territories, promoting religious and ethnic tolerance and developing healthy economic exchange." During the discussions, the secretary-general announced that the UN intended to increase its presence in Iraq by adding to staff already located in Erbil, a city in the north, and by creating a new southern office in Basra. Both Ban and al-Maliki commented to reporters that the meeting was a positive one. At a following news conference, the secretary-general said, "This meeting has helped to promote a stronger partnership between the international community and Iraq. The United Nations is committed to supporting this partnership."

CLIMATE CHANGE

Another subject Secretary-General Ban seems particularly passionate about is global warming. At a vast number of his many international meetings, Ban made certain to bring up the issue of climate change and its effects around the world. He also published an article in the *Washington Post* titled, "A Climate Culprit in Darfur." In this piece, he stated that "It is no accident that the violence in Darfur erupted during the drought," and then went on to highlight an article by Stephan Faris that appeared in the *Atlantic Monthly*. This article by Faris explained the roots of the violence in Darfur. Before the drought, nomadic Arab herders coexisted peacefully with the region's black farmers. Their relations were so friendly, in fact, that the farmers welcomed the herders as they traveled back and forth across the land and allowed their camels to graze, and gladly offered to share their wells. But when rain became scarce, the farmers fenced off their land to keep it from being ruined by the traveling herds. In the region's history, this was the first time there was not enough food and water for all. Eventually fighting broke out and escalated to the terrible conflict ongoing today. The drought in Darfur was related to failing rains in Sudan recorded by scientists 20 years ago. In his article, Ban said that UN statistics showed that the nation's average precipitation had declined by about 40 percent since the 1980s. At first scientists thought this was a quirk and nothing to be alarmed about. After further investigation, however, this reduction in rain was shown to be due in some part to global warming.

As a special effort, Ban called a high-level meeting to take place on September 24, the day before the General Assembly would meet for its next session. The gathering was intended to set the stage for another major meeting—the UN Framework Convention on Climate Change—to take place in December in Bali, Indonesia. There, Ban hoped to develop a new global climate treaty to follow the Kyoto Protocol adopted in 1997. The Kyoto agreement, which limits industrialized nations on the amount of carbon dioxide their factories and power plants can emit, will expire in 2012.

The secretary-general made preparations for the September gathering far in advance. Before a meeting set with George W. Bush in July, Ban announced to the press that he intended to ask the U.S. president to send a top official to the climate change meeting. This was an important move because the Bush administration had been opposed to the Kyoto Protocol. Later that same month, Ban also made a visit to San Francisco where he met with California governor Arnold Schwarzenegger, who has been at the forefront of the global warming issue in the United States and has helped pass legislation in his state to reduce emissions. During his trip, Ban toured local Bay Area businesses that use green technologies. At a breakfast with staff of the *San Francisco Chronicle*, the secretary-general told reporters, "I am not a scientist; I am not an economist, but if you ask any scientist or economist they will tell you the science is clear, the economies are clear. They say action should have been taken yesterday, but it may not be too late if we take it today."

At the end of July, Ban convened the General Assembly for a debate on the global challenge of climate change. In his address to the General Assembly, he said the week-long discussions would lay the groundwork for the meetings to occur in September and December. In the opening of his address to the delegates he said, "We meet at a time when climate change—long on the international agenda—is finally receiving the very highest attention that it merits. . . . The effects of these changes are already grave, and they are growing. . . . We cannot go on this way for long. We cannot continue with business as usual. The time has come for decisive action on a global scale." At this General Assembly meeting, the UN chief also announced his "Greening the UN" initiative, the purpose of which is to minimize the entire organization's own carbon footprint.

Ban's September meeting on global warming was attended by top officials from 80 countries, as well as former American vice president Al Gore and Governor Schwarzenegger. During the gathering, Ban stressed the urgent need to come up with a new treaty that would cut emissions by industrialized nations even further than the Kyoto treaty had done.

UN REFORM

Before Ban was even in the running for the job of secretary-general, the UN had been plagued by bad publicity that was shaking people's trust in the world organization. In Iraq, there had been the oil-for-food scandal. The UN oil-for-food program was set up in December 1996 as a humanitarian relief effort for the Iraqi people. It allowed Iraq to sell oil to buy food and medicine and repay war reparations stemming from its 1990 attack on Kuwait. In 2005, a man named Paul Volcker investigated the oil-for-food arrangement that had occurred in the 1990s. He concluded that the program, which had been intended for good, had actually been filled with waste and corruption. Further validation of the corruption came in January 2007, when the former executive director of the UN program, Benon V. Sevan of Cyprus, was indicted by a federal

Ban Ki-moon *(above center, in Antarctica)* has embraced his role as the leader of the UN and strives to maintain peace by combating emerging international problems, such as global warming. Since his swearing-in as UN secretary-general, Ban has implemented policies to modernize the international organization, and continues to strive toward his dream of world peace.

prosecutor. The charges included his acceptance of $160,000 in bribes. Benon was the third UN official to be either charged or convicted of crimes relating to the oil-for-food program. Upon federal prosecutors' announcement of Benon's indictment, Ban—in Washington, D.C., at the time—told *Washington Post* reporters that he was committed to raising the ethical standards of the UN and planned to "lead by example."

Then there was reported corruption in the UN's purchasing operations, and—perhaps worst of all—sexual abuse by UN peacekeepers. This last transgression was reported in the Democratic Republic of the Congo. There were allegations that some of the peacekeepers sent to protect the people of this nation had instead preyed on its children. Peacekeepers were accused of offering bananas, coins, or candy in exchange for sex. Some of the victims were as young as twelve.

Restoring Trust

"My first priority will be to restore trust," Ban said on December 14 in a speech after taking the oath of office. The South Korean did not waste any time in making good on his promise. Less than two weeks into office, Ban made history when he went public with his financial disclosure statement, something no secretary-general had ever done before. Now, people knew he was worth at the most $2.5 million. He hoped his action would be seen as part of the trust and confidence he hoped to restore in people's perception of the UN.

Another act during his first month as UN head was to ask all senior Secretariat officials (except those who had their positions as a result of input from other UN bodies), a total of about 60 people, to resign. Ban wanted to show that top UN jobs were not entitlements for either specific individuals or their nations of origin.

Upon taking office, the secretary-general laid out a plan of core tasks to take on in the area of UN reform. One was to strengthen the UN's three pillars—security, development, and human rights. Another was to breathe new life and inject new confidence into the Secretariat. Also on his list was the desire to improve human resource management and career development systems. Ban also sought to set the highest standards of ethics, professionalism, and accountability within the world organization. Finally, he hoped to usher in a renewed relationship between the Secretariat and member states.

Heading Off a New Scandal

In January 2007, a published report emerged on the UN Development Program in North Korea. According to the report, North Korea was making unaccountable cash payments to local staff members as well its own government, benefiting the regime of the nation's leader, Kim Jong Il, rather than its people. Promptly after meeting with Ad Melkert, associate administrator of the program, on January 19, Ban requested that an outside examination of all United Nations activities take place. This seemed to be a good step in heading off the types of scandals that had harmed the world body's reputation in previous years.

Gender Equality

Another aspect of UN reform that Ban wished to tackle was gender parity. In a United Nations Association magazine, the secretary-general was quoted on the recruitment of UN staff: "Gender-balancing, mainstreaming is a very important agenda not only for the United Nations but for all the international community. This is the area [where] we have to put emphasis." And Ban had already begun. After his election, he promised to place a woman from a developing country as second in command. At the end of his first week in office, Ban announced his selection of Tanzanian Asha-Rose Mtengeti-Migiro as deputy secretary-general. Migiro, who Ban said would be responsible for the day-to-day management of the organization, had served in her nation's cabinet for six years, most recently as Tanzania's foreign minister.

Ban reiterated his stance on equality on August 13, 2007, when he welcomed the first-ever entire female class of UN security officers. At an event in honor of the 12 women, the secretary-general said, "We need to be exemplary and to be the first organization to keep the internationally agreed commitment of having full gender balance."

STREAMLINING THE UN

Ban's promises before becoming secretary-general included making the world body a leaner and more efficient organization, stating that some of the problems were due to needs for consolidation and coordination that would reduce the overlap among various UN agencies. Even before his election as the new UN chief, Ban said during a speech in New York, "The UN should first reform itself. [It] suffers from its inability to set priorities and make choices. The UN needs to promise less and deliver more." Speaking publicly before meeting with his UN staff for the first time, Ban said, "My watchword will be meritocracy," which was a comment on fulfilling his promise to streamline the UN's complex bureaucracy.

THE FUTURE FOR BAN AND THE UN

In his first year alone, Ban embraced his role as leader of the UN, traveling around the globe to meet world leaders and taking action on numerous issues affecting the world's peoples. It is said that each individual secretary-general seems to define the role for himself. Ban appears to be setting the stage for a secretary-general as role model. He has worked hard to show people the benefits of diplomatic approaches in solving conflict; he has decried the neglect of people to change their ways of living in order to save the planet from global warming; and he has begun to set standards for other UN staff as the gateway to restoring people's trust in the organization. Ban's further success in these areas will no doubt help others to decide if the UN can remain relevant in an ever-growing and increasingly complex world and, perhaps more important, help to craft the future of the world in which we live.

CHRONOLOGY

1899 First International Peace Conference is held.

1904 Russo-Japanese War starts. It ends in 1905 with Korea becoming a Japanese protectorate.

1919 Paris Peace Conference is held, resulting in the Treaty of Versailles, which includes provisions for the creation of the League of Nations.

1942 During World War II, four world leaders sign the United Nations Declaration.

1944 **June 13** Ban Ki-moon is born in Eumseong, Korea.

1945 **June** After World War II, 50 nations meet for the United Nations Conference on International Organization.

August Korea is divided by the 38th parallel, separating the northern and the southern areas.

October 24 The United Nations officially begins its work.

1946 **February 1** The UN elects its first secretary-general, Trygve Lie.

April The UN's International Court of Justice begins in The Hague, Netherlands.

1948 The General Assembly proclaims the Universal Declaration of Human Rights.

1950 The Korean War begins.

1953 The Korean War ends and results in an armistice agreement creating the Demilitarized Zone separating North from South.

1961 The UN elects its first Asian secretary-general, U Thant.

1962 Ban wins an English-language contest and receives a trip to the United States, where he meets President John F. Kennedy.

1970 Ban earns a bachelor of arts degree in international relations from Seoul University.

1971 He marries high school sweetheart, Yoo Soon-taek.

1975 He begins a long career with the South Korean Foreign Ministry as a civil servant in its UN division.

1985 Ban finishes a master's degree in public administration at Harvard.

1991 South Korea becomes an official member state of the United Nations.

1994 The UN Trusteeship Council suspends activities after successfully helping all Trust Territories gain either self-governance or independence.

1998 Ban starts two years as the South Korean ambassador to Austria.

1999 Ban takes over as chair of the Preparatory Commission for the Comprehensive Nuclear-Test-Ban Treaty Organization.

2001 He steps in as chef de cabinet for the Korean UN General Assembly president and helps keep calm within the UN after the September 11 terrorist attacks in the United States.

2003 The conflict in Sudan's Darfur region begins.

2004 **January** Ban becomes South Korean foreign minister.

June Ban survives crisis as foreign minister when a South Korean translator in Iraq is captured and beheaded on video.

2005 **February 16** The UN's Kyoto Protocol takes effect in an effort to prevent further global warming.

September Ban helps secure a joint statement with North Korea in the Six-Party Talks meant to resolve the North Korean nuclear issue.

2006 **February** South Korea announces Ban's nomination for UN secretary-general.

July 24 The UN Security Council holds its first straw poll for nomination of secretary-general.

September 14 and 28 The Security Council conducts two more straw polls.

October 2 The Security Council holds its final straw poll.

October 9 The Security Council takes an official vote and nominates Ban to the General Assembly as secretary-general.

October 13 The General Assembly elects Ban as the UN's eighth secretary-general.

November Ban resigns as South Korean foreign minister.

2007 **January 1** Ban starts his term as secretary-general.

January 19 Ban requests an outside examination of all United Nations activities after a report suggests corruption may exist within the UN Development Program in North Korea.

January 27 Ban arrives in the Democratic Republic of the Congo as part of his first international trip as head of the UN.

January He participates in the African Union summit in Addis Ababa, Ethiopia.

February 16 Ban introduces the *Counter-Terrorism Online Handbook.*

March 22 Ban makes a surprise visit to Iraq and is interrupted during a press conference with Iraqi prime minister Nuri Kamal al-Maliki when a mortar attack strikes nearby.

June 4 Ban takes part in the opening session of the Organization of American States' 37th General Assembly in Panama.

June 8 Ban participates in the Group of Eight (G-8) summit in Germany.

September 3 Ban makes first trip to Sudan.

September 21 Ban announces changes to the roster of UN Messengers for Peace and also announces the creation of a trust fund to support future Darfur peace talks.

September 24 Ban calls together a high-level meeting on climate change the day before the General Assembly's opening session.

October 27 Peace talks on Darfur take place in Libya.

December Ban conducts the UN Framework Convention on Climate Change to create a new treaty to replace the Kyoto Protocol when it expires.

2008 Ban appeals for the senior leaders of Cambodia's murderous Khmer Rouge regime to be brought to justice.

Bibliography

Al Jazeera. "UN Chief Appoints Key Aides." January 1, 2007. Available online. http://english.aljazeera.net/news/americas/2007/01/2008525141824600160.html.

Associated Press. "Ban Ki-moon Takes the Reins of the UN." *Sydney Morning Herald.* January 1, 2007. Available online. http://www.smh.com.au/news/world/ban-kimoon-takes-the-reins-of-the-un/2007/01/01/1167500054341.html.

———. "Ban Ki-moon's First 100 Days." News24. October 4, 2007. Available online. http://www.news24.com/News24/World/News/0,,2-10-1462_2096063,00.html.

Avni, Benny. "In Interview, New U.N. Chief Sets New Path." *New York Sun.* December 26, 2006. Available online. http://www.nysun.com/pf.php?id=45703&v=5649660911.

Ban Ki-moon. "A Climate Crisis in Darfur." United Nations. June 16, 2007. Available online. http://www.un.org/sg/press_article_darfur.shtml.

———. "A Climate Culprit in Darfur." *Washington Post.* June 16, 2007. Available online. http://www.washingtonpost.com/wp-dyn/content/article/2007/06/15/AR2007061501857.html.

———. Address to General Assembly Thematic Debate: "Climate Change as a Global Challenge." UN News Centre. July 31, 2007. Available online. http://www.un.org/apps/news/infocus/sgspeeches/search_full.asp?statID=105.

———. "Statement on the Adoption of the Resolution on the Hybrid Force for Darfur." UN News Centre. July 31, 2007. Available online. http://www.un.org/apps/news/infocus/sgspeeches/search_full.asp?statID=107.

———. "What I Saw in Darfur: Untangling the Knots of a Complex Crisis." *Washington Post.* September 14,

2007. Available online. http://www.washingtonpost.com/wp-dyn/content/article/2007/09/13/AR2007091301680.html.

Bartelby.com. "Hague Conferences." *Columbia Encyclopedia*, 6th ed. Available online. http://www.bartleby.com/65/ha/HagueCon.html.

———. "Hague Tribunal." *Columbia Encyclopedia*, sixth edition. Available online. http://www.bartleby.com/65/ha/HagueTri.html.

BBC News. "Next UN Chief Pledges Key Reforms." November 10, 2006. Available online. http://news.bbc.co.uk/1/hi/world/asia-pacific/6134880.stm.

———. "Profile: Ban Ki-moon." Available online. http://news.bbc.co.uk/2/hi/asia-pacific/5401856.stm.

———. "Profile: United Nations." Available online. http://news.bbc.co.uk/1/hi/world/europe/country_profiles/3159028.stm.

———. "Q&A: How the UN Chief Is Chosen." September 28, 2006. Available online. http://news.bbc.co.uk/2/hi/5388220.stm.

Bolton, John R. "Don't Ban Your Instincts, Ban Ki-moon." *Washington Post.* January 14, 2007. Available online. http://www.washingtonpost.com/wp-dyn/content/article/2007/01/12/AR2007011202061.html.

Boston.com. "Ban Ki Moon." Available online. http://www.boston.com/news/world/asia/articles/2006/10/09/ban_ki _moon/.

Brouwer, Marina. "Ban Ki Moon—The Man Who Would Be UN Chief." Radio Netherlands. October 14, 2006. Available online. http://www.radionetherlands.nl/currentaffairs/kor061004.

Bruning, Karla. "A Refreshing Moment: Ban Ki-moon Is a Shoe-in to Succeed Kofi Annan at the United Nations. What Will Change?" *Newsweek.* October 3, 2006. Available online. http://www.newsweek.com/id/45201/page/2.

CBC News. "Ban Ki-moon Places 'Own Nuance' on Death Penalty Policy." January 3, 2007. Available online. http://www.cbc.ca/world/story/2007/01/02/bankimoon-darfur.html.

———. "Ban Ki-moon Poised to Be the Next Secretary-General." October 13, 2006. Available online. http://www.cbc.ca/news/background/un/kimoon.html.

CBS News. "U.N. Chief Urges U.S. to Stick by Iraqis." WCCO.com. July 17, 2007. Available online. http://wcco.com/politics/United.Nations.Secretary.2.286709.html.

CBS News/Associated Press. "U.N. Swears in New Secretary-General." December 14, 2006. Available online. http://www.cbsnews.com/stories/2006/12/14/world/main2265985.shtml?source=search_story.

Central Intelligence Agency. "The World Factbook: South Korea." Available online. https://www.cia.gov/library/publications/the-world-factbook/geos/ks.html.

CNN.com. "South Korean Foreign Minister Named Next U.N. Leader." Available online. http://www.cnn.com/2006/US/10/13/un.secretary.general.

Coultan, Mark. "Ban Ki-moon's Rising Star." *Sydney Morning Herald.* January 6, 2007. Available online. http://www.smh.com.au/news/world.

Council on Foreign Relations. "Restoring the Vitality of the United Nations." Transcript. May 31, 2006. Available online. http://www.cfr.org/publication/10833/restoring_

the_vitality_of_the_united_nations_rush_transcript_federal_news_service_inc.html?breadcrumb=%2Fpublication%2Fpublication_list%3Fgroupby%3D3%26type%3Dtranscript%26filter%3D2006%26page%3D5.

Crossette, Barbara. "Meet Your New Secretary-General: Ban Ki-moon." *The Interdependent.* Winter 2006–2007. Available online. http://www.theinterdependent.org.

Dam, Janie. "Background Essay: Timeline of North Korea's Nuclear Ambitions." AskAsia.org. 2006. Available online. http://www.askasia.org/teachers/essays/essay.php?np=146.

Economist. "The UN's New Secretary General: Enter Mr. Ban." October 5, 2006. Available online. http://www.economist.com/opinion.

Eyewitness to History. "The Sinking of the *Lusitania*, 1915." 2000. Available online. http://eyewitnesstohistory.com/snpwwi2.htm.

Fazio, Dalai. "Secretary-General Ban Ki-moon Arrives for First Day of Work." *UN Chronicle*, Online Edition. United Nations. Available online. http://www.un.org/Pubs/chronicle/2006/webArticles/010207_Ban.htm.

Fitzpatrick, Julia. "Ban's Darfur Moment (With More to Come)." Citizens for Global Solutions. July 17, 2007. Available online. http://globalsolutions.org/blog/index.php/home?s=ban%27s+darfur+moment&sentence=sentence&submit=Search.

Gordon, Amanda. "Out & About." *New York Sun.* January 24, 2007. Available online. http://www.nysun.com/article/47289.

Hauben, Ronda. "Ban Ki-moon's Role of UN Secretary General." OhmyNews International. June 30, 2007. Available online. http://english.ohmynews.com/articleview/article_view.asp?menu=c10400&no=369577&rel_no=1.

Herland, Neil. "Is Ban Ki-moon a Franco-Phoney?" CBC News. December 14, 2006. Available online. http://www.cbc.ca/news/reportsfromabroad/herland/20061214.html.

Hoge, Warren. "Afghan Hears Foreign Concerns on Drugs and Political Dialogue." *New York Times.* September 24, 2007. Available online. http://query.nytimes.com/gst/fullpage.html?res=9405EED71439F937A1575AC0A9619C8B63.

———. "For New U.N. Chief, a Past Misstep Leads to Opportunity." *New York Times.* December 9, 2006. Available online. http://www.nytimes.com/2006/12/09/world/asia/09ban.html.

———. "For United Nations Chief, a Business Trip Is Personal." *New York Times.* September 10, 2007. Available online. http://www.nytimes.com/2007/09/10/world/africa/10nations.html?_r=1&oref=login.

———. "In Sudan, U.N. Secretary-General Renews Peace Effort." *New York Times.* September 4, 2007. Available online. http://www.nytimes.com/2007/09/04/world/africa/04nations.html.

———. "Libyan Leader Says He Will Bring Rebels to Meeting on Darfur." *New York Times.* September 9, 2007. Available online. http://www.nytimes.com/2007/09/09/world/africa/09nations.html.

———. "Revisiting Issue, U.N. Chief Clarifies Death-Penalty Stance." *New York Times.* January 12, 2007. Available online. http://www.nytimes.com/2007/01/12/world/12nations.html.

———. "26 Nations Call for Sending U.N. Peacekeeping Force to Darfur." *New York Times.* September 22, 2007. Available online. http://query.nytimes.com/gst/

fullpage.html?res=9A0DE6D7113AF931A1575AC0A9619C8B63.

———. "U.N. Chief Isn't Discouraged by His Close Call in Iraq." *New York Times.* March 24, 2007. Available online. http://query.nytimes.com/gst/fullpage.html?res=980DE3DA1530F937A15750C0A9619C8B63.

———. "U.N. Chief Urges More Help for Iraq." September 23, 2007. *New York Times.* Available online. http://query.nytimes.com/gst/fullpage.html?res=9500EFD8173BF930A1575AC0A9619C8B63.

———. "U.N. to Audit Its Activities After Reports on North Korea Program." January 20, 2007. *New York Times.* Available online. http://www.nytimes.com/2007/01/20/world/asia/20nations.html.

Integrated Regional Information Networks. "Tough-Minded New U.N. Chief." Worldpress.org. November 29, 2006. Available online. http://www.worldpress.org/print_article.cfm?article_id=2702&dont=yes.

International Committee of the Red Cross. "International Humanitarian Law—Treaties and Documents: Final Act of the International Peace Conference." The Hague, July 29, 1899. Available online. http://www.icrc.org.

International Court of Justice. "The Court." Available online. http://www.icj-cij.org/court/index.php?p1=1&PHPSESSID=4c2842b9cfe0087b966e7549622cee9d.

JayanthaDhanapala.com. "Jayantha Dhanapala: Biography." Available online. http://jayanthadhanapala.com/biography.html.

Kirk, Donald. "The Quiet Diplomat Who May Lead the UN." *Christian Science Monitor.* October 3, 2006. Available online. http://www.csmonitor.com/2006/1003/p01s03-wogi.htm.

Kools, Frank. "South Korean Is Likely to Be New UN Chief." Radio Netherlands. March 10, 2006. Available online. http://www.radionetherlands.nl/currentaffairs/kor061003mc.

Korea.net. "Ban Departs Korean Foreign Ministry for Top U.N. Job." Gale International. November 11, 2006. Available online. http://www.songdo.com/default.aspx?p=1508&d=1145.

Lague, David. "Plan to Disarm North Korea Is Evaluated as Talks Recess." *New York Times.* October 1, 2007. Available online. http://query.nytimes.com/gst/fullpage.html?res=9806E4DA1739F932A35753C1A9619C8B63.

Lederer, Edith M. "U.N. Authorizes Darfur Spillover Force." September 25, 2007. My Wire. Available online. http://www.mywire.com/pubs/AP/2007/09/25/4570549?&pbl=222.

LeFranchi, Howard. "First Test for New UN Chief: Darfur." *Christian Science Monitor.* January 26, 2007. Available online. http://www.csmonitor.com/2007/0126/p03s02-woaf.htm.

Lekic, Slobodan. "Leaders Meet on Africa at U.N." *USA Today.* September 25, 2007. Available online. http://www.usatoday.com/news/world/2007-09-25-3365397592_x.htm.

Leopold, Evelyn. "Celebs New UN Peace Messengers." *Calgary Herald.* September 24, 2007. Available online. http://www.canada.com/victoriatimescolonist/news/life/story.html?id=5e38011a-c1d5-4517-92fa-9b8e3c52a3a0.

———. "U.N. Chief Warns of Daunting Challenges in World." Reuters. September 25, 2007. Available online. http://www.reuters.com/article/newsOne/idUSN2537316720070925.

Lynch, Colum. "Former U.N. Oil-for-Food Chief Indicted." *Washington Post.* January 17, 2007. Available online.

http://www.washingtonpost.com/wp-dyn/content/article/2007/01/16/AR2007011600706.html.

———. "U.N. Chief Calls for 'Real Breakthrough' on Climate Change." *Washington Post.* September 25, 2007. Available online. http://www.washingtonpost.com/wp-dyn/content/article/2007/09/24/AR2007092400128.html.

MacAskill, Ewen, Ed Pilkington, and Jon Watts. "Despair at UN Over Selection of 'Faceless' Ban Ki-moon as General Secretary." October 7, 2006. *Guardian.* Available online. http://www.guardian.co.uk/print/0,,329595185-104490,00.html.

Mallaby, Sebastian, and Paul A. Volcker. "Why New U.N. Chief Is Bound to Fail." Council on Foreign Relations. February 26, 2007. Available online. http://www.cfr.org/publication/12728/why_new_un_chief_is_bound_to_fail.html.

McCormack, Sean, spokesman. "Joint Statement of the Fourth Round of the Six-Party Talks Beijing, September 19, 2005." U.S. Department of State. September 19, 2005. Available online. http://www.state.gov/r/pa/prs/ps/2005/53490.htm.

National Office for Climate Change and Ozone Protection. "U.N. Chief Will Ask President George W. Bush to Give Top Level Support to U.N. Meeting on Climate Change." July 27, 2007. Available online. http://www.noccop.org.vn/modules.php?name=Airvariable_protec&op=ndetail&n=315&nc=7.

New York Times. "The Reach of War: Hostage: Seoul to Send Troops to Iraq Despite Kidnapping." June 21, 2004. Available online. http://query.nytimes.com/gst/fullpage.html?res=9903EED91239F932A15755C0A9629C8B63.

New Zealand Herald. "UN Braced for Change as New Boss Takes Over." January 2, 2007. Available online. http://www.

nzherald.co.nz/topic/story.cfm?c_id=467&objectid=10417444.

O'Driscoll, Sean. *The Washington Diplomat.* November 2006. Available online. http://www.washdiplomat.com/November%202006/a3_11_06b.html.

PBS. "American Experience: Woodrow Wilson." Available online. http://www.pbs.org/wgbh/amex/wilson/.

Pisik, Betsy. "U.N. Report: Ban Ki-moon to Be Sworn In." World Peace Herald. Available online. http://wpherald.com/articles/2488/1/UN-Report-Ban-Ki-moon-to-be-sworn-in/Bans-unexpectedly-funny-appearance.html.

Porter, Keith. "Who Is Ban Ki-moon?" The Stanley Foundation. Available online. http://www.stanleyfoundation.org/articles.cfm?id=5.

Preston, Julia. "New U.N. Chief Invites Controversy by Declining to Oppose Hussein Execution." *New York Times.* January 3, 2007. Available online. http://www.nytimes.com/2007/01/03/world/middleeast/03nations.html?_r=1&oref=slogin.

———. "Tanzanian Woman Is Chosen for U.N.'s 2nd Highest Post." *New York Times.* January 6, 2007. Available online. http://www.nytimes.com/2007/01/06/world/06nations.html?_r=1&oref=slogin.

Reuters. "New UN Leader Starts Work." *Sydney Morning Herald.* January 3, 2007. Available online. http://www.smh.com/au/news/world.

Semple, Kirk. "As U.N. Chief Meets Premier of Iraq, the Zone Is Shelled." *New York Times.* March 23, 2007. Available online. http://www.nytimes.com/2007/03/23/world/middleeast/23iraq.html.

Shaikh, Nermeen. "AsiaSource Interview with South Korean Foreign Minister Ban Ki-moon." September 26, 2006. AsiaSource. Available online. http://www.asiasource.org/news/special_reports/kimoon.cfm.

Shawn, Eric. "Travels with Ban Ki-moon." February 3, 2007. FoxNews. Available online. http://www.foxnews.com/printer_friendly_story/0,3566,247799,00.html.

Stritof, Sheri, and Bob Stritof. "Ban Ki-moon and Yoo Soon-taek Marriage Profile." About.com. Available online. http://marriage.about.com/od/politics/p/bankimoon.htm.

Sudanese Media Center. "Korean Foreign Affairs and Trade Minister Visits Sudan." Available online. http://www.smc.sd/en/artopic.asp?artID=12695&aCK=EJ.

Sullivan, John. "U.N. Approves Peacekeepers for Darfur." *New York Times*. August 1, 2007. Available online. http://www.nytimes.com/2007/08/01/world/africa/01nations.html?_r=1&oref=slogin.

Time. "Dashboard—The Map: How Armies of Peace Are Deployed." July 23, 2007: 16.

Times Online. "Profile: Ban Ki-moon, Frontrunner for the Top UN Job." September 29, 2006. Available online. http://www.timesonline.co.uk/tol/news/world/article655125.ece.

Trevelyan, Laura. "Darfur Challenge for Ban Ki-moon." BBC News. February 1, 2007. Available online. http://news.bbc.co.uk/go/pr/fr/-/2/hi/africa/6319359.stm.

UN Chronicle. "The Eighth Secretary-General of the UN: A Top Administrator and Disarmament Expert Takes the Helm." United Nations. Available online. http://www.un.org/Pubs/chronicle/2006/issue4/0406p04.htm.

UNICEF. "United Nations Reform: UN Secretary-General Ban Ki-moon Begins His Tenure in Office." January 2, 2007. Available online. http://www.unicef.org/unreform/index_37936.html?q=printme.

United Nations Web site. Available online. http://www.un.org.

UN News Centre. Available online. http://www.un.org.

U.S. Department of State, Bureau of Public Affairs. "U.S. Financial Contributions to the United Nations System." Available online. http://www.state.gov/documents/organization/92734.pdf.

U.S. Department of State, Office of the Press Secretary. "Statement by the President on Agreement Announced at Six-Party Talks." October 3, 2007. Available online. http://www.state.gov/p/eap/rls/prs/2007/93212.htm.

U.S. Department of State, Office of the Spokesman. "Six Parties October 3, 2007 Agreement on 'Second-Phase Actions for the Implementation of the Joint Statement.'" October 3, 2007. Available online. http://www.state.gov/r/pa/prs/2007/oct/93223.htm.

Voice of America News. "U.N. to Open New Office in Baghdad." August 21, 2003. Available online. http://voanews.com/english/archive/2003-08/a-2003-08-21-29-UN.cfm.

Wadhams, Nick. "Ban Ki-moon Cements Hold on U.N. Post." Boston.com. October 2, 2006. Available online. http://www.boston.com/news/world/asia/.

Walsh, Bryan. "The Man Who Would Be Kofi." *Time*. September 29, 2006. Available online. http://www.time.com/time/world/article/0,8599,1540999,00.html.

———. "The Teflon Diplomat." *Time.* October 9, 2006. Available online. http://www.time.com/time/magazine/article/0,9171,501061016-1544009,00.html.

"Who Is Ban Ki-moon?" News24. October 10, 2006. Available online. http://www.news24.com/News24/World/News/0,,2-10-1462_2010614,00.html.

Winik, Lyric Wallwork. "Can Ban Ki-moon Save the UN?" *Parade.* June 24, 2007: 6–7.

Xinhua. "Interview: Ban Ki-moon Vows to Focus on Secretariat Reform, Trust-Building." People's Daily Online. Available online. http://english.people.com.cn/20061216_333268.html.

Yi, Matthew. "U.N. Chief's Mission to Novato: Secretary-General Ban Ki-moon, Visiting San Francisco to Address the Problems of Our Time, First Will Take Time Out to Visit a Valued Friend." *San Francisco Chronicle.* July 26, 2007.

Zissis, Carin. "Backgrounder: The Role of the UN Secretary-General." Council on Foreign Relations. January 5, 2007. Available online. http://www.cfr.org/publication/12348/role_of_the_un_secretarygeneral.html?breadcrumb=%2Fpublication%2Fpublication_list%3Fgroupby%3D3%26type%3Dbackgrounder%26filter%3D2007%26page%3D5.

FURTHER READING

BOOKS

Andersen, Stephen O., K. Madhava Sarma, and Lani Sinclair. *Protecting the Ozone Layer: The United Nations History.* London: Earthscan Publications, 2002.

Boudreau, Thomas E. *Sheathing the Sword: The U.N. Secretary-General and the Prevention of International Conflict* (Contributions in Political Science). Westport, Conn.: Greenwood Press, 1991.

Chesterman, Simon, ed. *Secretary or General?: The UN Secretary-General in World Politics.* New York: Cambridge University Press, 2007.

Doyle, Michael W., and Nicholas Sambanis. *Making War and Building Peace: United Nations Peace Operations.* Princeton, NJ: Princeton University Press, 2006.

Fasulo, Linda. *An Insider's Guide to the UN.* New Haven, Conn.: Yale University Press, 2005.

Kennedy, Paul. *The Parliament of Man: The Past, Present, and Future of the United Nations.* Reprint edition. New York: Vintage, 2007.

Kim, Ju. *The Development of Modern South Korea* (Routledge Advances in Korean Studies). New York: Routledge, 2006.

Mingst, Karen A. *The United Nations in the Twenty-First Century* (Dilemmas in World Politics). Boulder, Colo.: Westview Press, 2006.

Pérez de Cuéllar, Javier. *Pilgrimage for Peace: A Secretary General's Memoir.* New York: Palgrave Macmillan, 1997.

United Nations. *Basic Facts About the United Nations.* New York: United Nations, 2004.

Weiss, Thomas J., and Sam Daws, eds. *The Oxford Handbook on the United Nations.* New York: Oxford University Press, 2007.

WEB SITES

CyberSchoolBus: United Nations—Global Teaching and Learning Project
http://www.un.org/pubs/cyberschoolbus/index.shtml

Korea.net: Gateway to Korea
http://www.korea.net/

United Nations
http://www.un.org

United Nations Peacekeeping 1948–2007: Timeline of UN Operations
http://www.un.org/depts/dpko/dpko/timeline/

United Nations Secretary-General
http://www.un.org/sg/

Photo Credits

page:

3: AP Images, Frank Franklin II
15: AP Images
18: © Bettmann/CORBIS
22: © Bettmann/CORBIS
26: AP Images
31: AP Images
34: AP Images
39: AP Images, Beth A. Keiser
45: © Foreign Ministry/ Handout/Reuters/Corbis
49: AP Images, Ahn Young-Joon
52: AP Images, Mark Garten
57: AP Images, Frank Franklin II
63: AP Images
68: AP Images, David Karp
77: AP Images, Mark Garten
81: AP Images, John Bompengo
85: AP Images
89: © Philip Dhil/epa/Corbis
93: © AP Images, Alfred de Montesquiou
100: © Eskinder Debebe/UN Handout/epa/Corbis

INDEX

About the Authors

REBECCA ALDRIDGE has been a writer and editor for more than 12 years. In addition to this title, she has written several nonfiction books for children, the most recent of which is *The Sinking of the Titanic* for Chelsea House. As an editor, she has had input on more than 50 children's books covering such diverse topics as breast cancer, vegetarianism, and tattooing and body piercing. She lives in Minneapolis, Minnesota.

ARTHUR SCHLESINGER, JR. is remembered as the leading American historian of our time. He won the Pulitzer Prize for his books *The Age of Jackson* (1945) and *A Thousand Days* (1965), which also won the National Book Award. Schlesinger was the Albert Schweitzer Professor of the Humanities at the City University of New York and was involved in several other Chelsea House projects, including the series *Revolutionary War Leaders*, *Colonial Leaders*, and *Your Government.*